TOUGH
TOPICS

TOUGH TOPICS

KELLY K

 CHARISMA HOUSE

For more resources like this, visit MyCharismaShop.com and the author's website at kellykministries.com.

Cataloging-in-Publication Data is on file with the Library of Congress.
International Standard Book Number: 978-1-63641-444-7
E-book ISBN: 978-1-63641-445-4

1 2024
Printed in the United States of America

Most Charisma Media products are available at special quantity discounts for bulk purchase for sales promotions, premiums, fund-raising, and educational needs. For details, call us at (407) 333-0600 or visit our website at charismamedia.com.

I would like to dedicate this book to my beautiful wife, Lindsay. You never stopped believing with me. I love you.

-«««•»»»-

"An excellent wife who can find? She is far more precious than jewels."
—Proverbs 31:10, ESV

CONTENTS

PREFACE

L ET ME START this book by expressing my deepest gratitude. Thank you for allowing me the opportunity to guide you in better understanding the Bible. Whether this is your first time engaging with Scripture or you're a seasoned reader looking for fresh insights, I want you to know that I don't take this responsibility lightly. It is a privilege and an honor to share what I've learned with you, and I approach this endeavor with great humility and care.

Before you begin reading this book, I want you to know I have covered it in prayer, both for the words within these pages and for you, the reader. I've sought God's wisdom, understanding, and discernment for every subject discussed here. I truly believe that as you read through these chapters, God will ignite a fresh fire in your heart, drawing you closer to Him and giving you a deeper appreciation for His Word.

However, there is something crucial I need to mention before we go any further. This book contains my personal interpretation of Scripture. I wrote each of these chapters the way I would want someone to explain these topics to me. Now, I recognize that we all come from different backgrounds, churches, and traditions. You may not agree with everything I present here, and that's OK. Perhaps the church you attend teaches certain things differently. Perhaps you were raised in a family that held different beliefs. Whatever the case may be, I want you to keep in mind one very important point: We are still on the same team. At the heart of it all, we share the same foundation of faith in Christ, even if our perspectives on certain topics differ.

One thing you can be assured of is that nothing in this book will contradict the core principles of God's Word or challenge the essential tenets of Christianity. I firmly believe in staying faithful to the Scriptures. However, some of the topics we will tackle are not straightforward or easy to explain. In many cases there isn't a single, clear-cut answer provided in the Bible. This is why we have to approach Scripture as a whole—as a mosaic, if you will. To arrive at thoughtful conclusions on these complex issues, we must consider the broader context of the Bible, pulling together verses and teachings from multiple books and chapters. This is where personal interpretation comes into play, as different people may arrive at different conclusions based on their own studies of and experiences with Scripture.

Allow me to illustrate this concept with a simple analogy. I do *not* like bananas. I don't like eating them, nor do I enjoy anything flavored like them. You could offer me the ripest, healthiest, most beautifully grown banana, and I still wouldn't touch it! Now, does my personal distaste for bananas make them bad? Absolutely not! It simply means that *I* don't like them. The same principle can apply when we approach certain teachings from Scripture. You may come across a teaching in this book and think, "I don't like this," or, "This doesn't align with what I was taught growing up." You may even feel that it contradicts the way your current pastor or church teaches the subject. And that's perfectly natural.

But here's the challenge I want to extend to you: Don't dismiss something just because you don't like it. Just as my dislike for bananas doesn't mean they aren't good, your initial reaction to a teaching doesn't necessarily mean it's incorrect. As followers of Christ, we must be willing to challenge our own preferences and biases with the Word of God. Even if a teaching isn't to your liking, but you find that it aligns with Scripture, I urge you to continue reading with an open heart and an open mind. It's possible that God has something He wants to reveal to you through it, even if it's presented in a way you're not accustomed to.

We all need to remain teachable. It's essential for our spiritual growth. After all, healthy things grow, and a key aspect of growth is being willing to learn about, adapt to, and refine our understanding of God's Word over time.

I don't claim to have everything figured out. In fact, I am far from that. The Bible is an inexhaustible source of wisdom, and I, as you are, am continually learning and growing. What I can promise you, however, is that I have done my absolute best to provide honest, biblically grounded responses to some of the most challenging questions that arise in the Christian faith. These are questions we all face at some point in our journeys with Jesus, and I pray that the answers and insights provided in this book bring you clarity, peace, and deeper understanding.

One of my greatest hopes for this book is that it will be a blessing to you. I hope it answers some of the difficult questions that may have weighed on your heart for some time. I hope it equips you with knowledge and understanding that you can share with your family, friends, and community. But more than anything, I pray that this book will spark a hunger in you for God's Word like never before. As good as this book may or may not be, it is no substitute for the Bible itself. Consider this book an appetizer to the feast that is God's Word. I am merely the server, presenting you with what I've learned, but God is the chef, and His Word is always the most satisfying meal you will ever partake in.

Enjoy! Love to you all.

CHAPTER 1

Out of All Religions, How Do We Know Christianity Is the Right One?

I N TODAY'S WORLD there are countless religions and belief systems, all claiming to offer the right path to truth, happiness, or spiritual fulfillment. If you've ever found yourself asking, "How do I know I've made the right choice? What if I've believed in the wrong faith or followed a false path?" you're not alone.

This is a very common question, and it's one that many people struggle with as they navigate their spiritual journeys. I'd like to share with you some thoughts that I believe the Holy Spirit revealed to me when I was wrestling with similar doubts.

First and foremost, it's crucial to understand that the Christian faith is rooted in proven historical events. The stories in the Bible aren't just allegories or myths; they are accounts of real events that have been historically documented and verified. This is a critical point that sets Christianity apart from most other religions. While many other belief systems rely on personal, unverifiable experiences or revelations, Christianity is based on public events that were witnessed and recorded. It's important to recognize that no other religion offers this kind of verifiable, historical foundation.

Let's take, for example, Islam.

The core of the Islamic faith is based on the belief that the prophet Muhammad received revelations from God. However, these revelations were private encounters that Muhammad alone experienced, and the rest of the world is asked to just *accept* his account of these events without any independent verification. There are no historical records, no public testimony, and no evidence outside Muhammad's own word to substantiate these claims. As a result, followers of Islam are required to accept these revelations on blind faith!

"You had a dream, and now you wrote a book, and we should all follow you? Oh, absolutely! I am *so* in!"

That's ridiculous, right?

Similarly, other Eastern religions such as Buddhism and Hinduism don't even attempt to anchor their beliefs in historical events. Their teachings are more philosophical or spiritual in nature, offering guidance on how to live life, without any historical claims that can be examined or verified. For instance, in Buddhism the focus is on the teachings of the Buddha, not on any miraculous, historical event that can be independently corroborated. Likewise, Hinduism offers a vast array of gods, beliefs, and practices, but again, there is no emphasis on historically verifiable events.

Christianity, however, is based on the life, death, and

resurrection of Jesus Christ—which were all *public* events. Jesus conducted a public ministry, healing the sick, performing miracles, and preaching to large crowds. His crucifixion took place publicly, in full view of many witnesses. After His death He was buried in a tomb that was well-known to the public, and three days later He rose from the dead and appeared to numerous people. These post-resurrection appearances were not private experiences that one or two people claimed to have had. Instead, Jesus appeared to individuals, small groups, and even large gatherings. The apostle Paul, writing in 1 Corinthians 15:6, refers to Jesus appearing after His resurrection to more than five hundred people at one time. This isn't the kind of claim that can easily be dismissed as false or a lie, especially considering that many of these witnesses were still alive when the New Testament was written.

The historical nature of Christianity is one of the key reasons it stands out from other religions. No other faith can claim that its core beliefs are based on publicly verifiable events that were witnessed by hundreds of people. While other religions ask you to trust in private revelations, Christianity presents a faith founded on public testimony and historical documentation. This is not to say that faith isn't required in Christianity; of course faith is essential. But it's a faith grounded in evidence, not blind trust in someone's private experience.

Another point worth considering is the degree to which Christianity is targeted and attacked by the world. Ask yourself: Why is Christianity, out of all the world's religions, the one that faces constant opposition and criticism? Why do so many people go out of their way to discredit the Bible, mock Christian beliefs, and even persecute Christians? You don't see this same level of hostility directed at other religions. The Bible is the most targeted and criticized book in history.

Why is that?

If the Bible were just another book, why would it provoke such strong reactions? If Christianity were just one of many belief systems, why would it be singled out for such intense opposition? The answer is simple. We have something the others don't! There's something different about Christianity, and deep down the world knows it. Satan, our spiritual enemy, knows it too. The Bible tells us we have an enemy who "prowls around like a roaring lion," seeking whom he may devour (1 Pet. 5:8). Satan hates the truth, and he especially hates the truth that is found in Jesus Christ.

Satan doesn't need to target dead religious belief systems that have no real power or influence. He focuses his attacks on what is alive, what is powerful, and what poses a threat to his plans. Christianity is alive because the Word of God is both living and active (Heb. 4:12). Christians who are filled with the Holy Spirit are forces to be reckoned with because they carry within them the power and presence of the risen Christ. That's why Satan targets Christianity so fiercely. He knows the power that resides in believers, and he's terrified of it.

Let me give you an analogy. Imagine you're a hunter and you come across a deer that's already dead. Are you going to waste your time shooting that deer? Of course not. You're looking for something that's alive and poses a challenge. In the same way, Satan doesn't bother attacking people or religions that pose no threat to him. But Christianity? That's a different story. Satan sees the power of Jesus Christ in the lives of believers, and he knows that this is the same power that *already* defeated him! That's why he works so hard to deceive, discourage, and destroy Christians. He's not concerned with other religions, because they don't pose a threat to his kingdom of darkness.

As Christians we need to be aware of the fact that we are in a spiritual battle.

The attacks we face, whether they come in the form of persecution, doubt, or temptation, are not random. They are the enemy's attempts to weaken our faith and keep us from living out the full potential of our relationship with Christ. But here's the good news: We don't fight this battle alone! Jesus Christ is with us every step of the way. He has already won the ultimate victory over sin, death, and the devil, and because of that, we can stand firm in our faith, knowing that the power of God is on our side.

One of the most beautiful aspects of Christianity is that it offers not just a set of beliefs but also a personal relationship with God Himself. This is something that sets us apart from other religions. I can personally testify to the reality of this relationship. I know Jesus Christ. I talk to Him every day, and He talks to me. I experience His presence in my life in tangible ways. I've seen Him heal, provide for, guide, and comfort not only me but also so many others in ways that cannot be explained by anything other than His real, active involvement in our lives.

However, I have never heard testimonies like that from people of any other religion. While other faiths may offer philosophical insights or moral teachings, they don't offer the kind of personal relationship with the living God that Christianity does. Jesus is alive, and He desires to have a relationship with each and every one of us. He's not distant or disconnected. He's intimately involved in our lives, and He wants us to experience His love, grace, and power on a daily basis.

If you've never experienced this kind of relationship with God, I encourage you to seek Him with all your heart. The Bible promises that if we seek God, we will find Him (Jer. 29:13). Pray to Him, ask Him to reveal Himself to you, and open your heart to the possibility that He is real, is alive, and wants to know you personally. God desires a relationship with you even more than you desire one with Him. He loves you, and He's waiting for you to turn to Him.

In conclusion, if you're still unsure about your faith or are wondering whether you've chosen the right path, I urge you to consider the evidence. Christianity is a faith grounded in historical events, not private revelations or unverifiable experiences. It's a faith that has withstood centuries of opposition and persecution and yet continues to grow and thrive because it is alive with the power of the living God. If you're still uncertain, pray. Ask God to reveal Himself to you, and I have no doubt that He will lead you to the truth. And that truth, my friend, is Jesus Christ, the one true God.

CHAPTER 2

How Do We Pray Correctly?

OW DO WE pray correctly? Is there a certain way, style, or format that works best? Why does it seem as if God is so quick to answer prayers for some people and so slow to answer them for others? Is it something we're doing wrong? For this topic I want to start by asking you a question. And I really want you to think about it for a minute.

Let's say, hypothetically, that you got into some financial trouble and had to take your favorite possession to the pawn shop. Now, while your item is in that pawn shop, no matter how bad you want it, you have no access to it. It's locked up. But let's also say that I see you going through all this. And because I love you, I go down to the pawn shop and pay off that debt for you. I drive straight to your house and tell you, "I love you so much! It broke my heart to see you going through this difficult time. So I went and paid the debt for you. You now have access to the thing you want."

Now here is the question I wanted you to think about: How ridiculous would it be if you showed up at my house every day after that, knocking on the door, begging me to give you your favorite possession back? "Kelly, you said you bought it back and paid for it, so can I have it, please? Will you give it to me? I really need it!" I mean, we both agree that's *ridiculous*, right? At some point I would have to say to you, "It's already been bought and paid for. You don't have to beg me for it. Just go *get it*."

That right there is what we do to God every single day.

Please hear me and understand this: There are two things that God will never do—what He has already done and what He has asked *you* to do. And that is the problem. It is so easy for us to forget what He has already done for us. So let me remind you today. When Jesus went to the cross, He didn't just pay for your salvation. In fact, the Greek word for *salvation* used in the New Testament is *sozo*, which means saved, healed, and delivered. It means all three! When you read the New Testament and see the word *healed*, it's *sozo*. When you see the word *salvation*, it's *sozo*. When you see the word *delivered*, it's *sozo*. What that tells us is that all three are connected as one. You can't have the saving without the healing. And you can't have the healing without the deliverance.

To break this down even further, when Jesus went to the cross, He didn't just pay for your salvation; He also paid for your healing and your deliverance—and your marriage, and your kids, and your job, and your health, and your finances, and your joy, and your peace, and your...

Are you getting it? He paid for it all! And since it all has been bought and paid for, you don't have to beg

God for anything. But that's what we do—isn't it? The majority of prayers from the majority of Christians are just us begging and pleading with God to do or give to us what His Word says He already did or already gave.

Ouch. Are you starting to see why some people pray with power and some don't? There is a huge difference in a prayer from a believer versus a prayer from a beggar. We each need to get to a place where we finally realize that everything we need or want from God has *already* been bought and paid for! Jesus did that for you.

One of the greatest revelations I've ever had is that I don't have to beg God for what I need; all I have to do is *thank* Him for it, because even though I don't see it yet, it's already been bought for me. The real question for every single one of us needs to be, Am I a beggar, or am I a believer?

If you are asking yourself that question right now, wondering which one you are, there is a very simple test you can take that will reveal exactly which one you are: Let me hear you pray. Your prayers are telling everyone around you, you, and God which one you are. A beggar prayer and a believer prayer sound very different. A beggar prayer sounds like this: "God, if You could, please heal my cousin Jimmy. God, if it be Your will, we need help with our finances this month. God, if it's not too much trouble, lead my sister Jenny to salvation. If You could...please...if it be Your will..."

A believer's prayer, though, sounds much different. A believer's prayer will sound something like this: "Father,

I *thank You* that two thousand years ago, Your Son, Jesus, paid for Jimmy's healing on the cross, and we receive it today in Jesus' name. God, I *thank You* that You are my provider, that Your Word says You see my needs coming before I do, and that You have *already* made a way for me. My cup runs over, and I know You will provide more than enough for me so I can also be a blessing to those around me. Father, I *thank You* that my sister Jenny's heart is turning toward You today. *Thank You* for putting people in her life to speak truth to her, and I *thank You* that she will receive it. In Jesus' name, devil, you don't get my sister!"

Do you see the difference? Do you *feel* the difference? If you start to remove the word *please* from your prayers and replace it with *thank you*, your prayer life will level up! "Well, wait a minute there, Kelly, I'm not going to *not* say please. That's just rude." OK, I hear what you're saying, but hear what I'm saying too. When I say thank you, it implies that the please is already there. I'm honoring God by saying thank you because He told me to speak in faith! When we thank Him for what He's done, even though we don't see it yet, that is how we use and exercise our faith. We are saying, "God, this is what I believe about You. I may not see it in my life yet, but I know who You are, and I know what You bought and paid for on behalf of me."

I have a nine-year-old son named Jaxx, and every single day after school, he and his friends run through my house and just beg me for snacks and drinks all afternoon. "Dad! Can we have some cookies? Can we have some juice? Can we please, Dad? *Please!*" These kids wear me out with the begging. But I also have a twenty-year-old daughter named Avery. I can't even begin to tell you how many times I've come home while Avery and her friends have every bit of food I've ever bought out on the counter—baking cookies, brownies, lasagna...whatever. And she didn't ask me at all!

So what is the difference? The difference is that Avery has a revelation of who her father is. And if her father bought and paid for it, it's in the pantry, and she has access to it. She knows, "I don't have to beg my dad for this food; I don't have to go and say, 'Please, can I eat some of your food?'" She knows she can just go get it, eat it, and enjoy it, and all she has to say to me is "Thank you, Dad!" because she knows how much I love her and that if I bought it, it's not just for me; she has access because I have access.

You see, for you to move from beggar to believer, you need better understanding and revelation of who your Father is. The truth is, your Father loves you more than anything. He loves you so much that He gave His one and only Son as the ultimate sacrifice so you would never have a single need in your life. That's who your Father is!

Every single promise in the Bible belongs to you. But those promises are not automatic. You have to go get them. "Well, how do we do that, Kelly?" It's actually easier than you think. The reason a believer's prayer is so powerful is that a believer prays God's Word back to Him. That's how you go get the promises of God. If you see God do it for one in the Bible, He'll do it for you. If the Bible says it, you can have it. You just have to start thanking God for what you see in the Bible that you *want* to see in your life. That, my friend, is called *faith*!

So let me encourage you today.

Do an evaluation of your prayer life today. Listen to the words you speak as you pray. Are you a beggar? Or are you a *believer*? Stop begging God for what He *already* bought and paid for—for you. Change the word *please* in your prayers to *thank you*, and just watch how God starts to move in your life!

CHAPTER 3

Is It OK for Christians
to Use Curse Words?

As CHRISTIANS IS it acceptable for us to cuss a little? It's a question many believers ask, and I'm sure you've heard arguments from both sides. On one hand, there are those who strongly oppose it, saying things like "No profanity! Talking like that is going to send you straight to hell." On the other hand, there are those who downplay the seriousness of using bad language, arguing, "God looks at our hearts. He knows I love Him, and these are just words. It's no big deal." I have even seen a guy come to see me preach not long ago who was in a T-shirt that said, "I love Jesus, but I cuss a little."

But let's take a step back from cultural attitudes and opinions for a moment and ask the more important question: What does the Bible say about cussing and the words we use?

One place we can start is Colossians 3:1. This chapter opens with an exhortation that sets the tone for the rest of this discussion: "Since you have been raised to new life with Christ, set your sights on the realities of heaven, where Christ sits in the place of honor at God's right hand" (NLT). This call to focus on heavenly things instead of earthly things should change our perspectives. As we shift our focus from this world to eternity, it is our job to bring heaven to earth. So instead of asking, "Is it OK to use profanity?" why not ask, "Will we be using profanity in heaven?"

"Heck yeah, bro!"

Um, I don't think so.

The answer is obviously a resounding no. And if we won't be using profanity in heaven for all eternity, why would we think it's fine to use those words here?

It's difficult to imagine any kind of profane or inappropriate language in a place where everything is holy and pure. And the reason for this becomes even clearer as we continue to read through Colossians 3. A few verses later we encounter this instruction: "So put to death the sinful, earthly things lurking within you" (v. 5, NLT). Then, verses 7–8 say, "You used to do these things when your life was still part of this world. But now is the time to get rid of anger, rage, malicious behavior, slander, and dirty language" (NLT).

That's a pretty direct statement, right? The Bible is telling us here that while profanity may have been acceptable in our old lives before knowing Christ, now that we belong to Him, it's time to put away *dirty language.*

But there are always counterarguments. I've heard people say things like "No, Kelly, it's the culture that defines what words are inappropriate. Therefore, if you grew up in America, you understand certain words and exactly what they mean and imply. But a word that may be considered offensive here may not be a curse word in another country. So this passage isn't really talking about our modern curse words."

And others argue, "We're not actually cursing anyone. Some of our swear words just have regular meanings, like the one that can refer to a donkey. So it's no big deal."

These are real responses I've heard when teaching about this topic, and I can totally understand what people are trying to say. However, we must continue to seek the truth from the Word of God. Let's turn to another key passage, Ephesians 4:29, which says, "Don't use foul or abusive language. Let everything you say be good and helpful, so that your words will be an encouragement to those who hear them" (NLT).

Now, this verse is incredibly important because it gives us a litmus test for the words we use. When we choose to use curse words or any kind of profanity, we should ask ourselves, "Are these words good and helpful? Are they encouraging to those around me?" The core principle here is that our words should always be uplifting, especially within the body of Christ. By their very nature, curse words and foul language are the opposite of uplifting; they are negative, filthy, and often degrading.

But we're not done yet.

Ephesians 5:4 takes it even further: "Let there be no filthiness nor foolish talk nor crude joking, which are out of place, but instead let there be thanksgiving" (ESV). Notice what this verse is doing. It's not just saying, "Don't use dirty language." It's telling us what to replace that kind of talk with—thanksgiving!

This idea of replacing bad language with something positive is incredibly powerful. In fact, the Bible tells us in Psalm 100:4 that we enter God's presence with thanksgiving: "Enter his gates with thanksgiving, and his courts with praise!" (ESV). There is something about giving thanks with our words that draws us closer to God. When we choose to use our mouths to give thanks rather than speak inappropriately, we are actively drawing near to God. And James 4:8 promises us that when we draw near to God, He draws near to us.

Consider also what Psalm 19:14 says: "Let the words of my mouth and the meditation of my heart be acceptable in your sight, O LORD, my rock and my redeemer" (ESV). This is a prayer for our words and thoughts to be pleasing to God. It's about aligning both what we think and what we say with God's will. Jesus echoes a similar principle in Luke 6:45: "The good person out of the good treasure of his heart produces good, and the evil person out of his evil treasure produces evil, for out of the abundance of the heart his mouth speaks" (ESV).

This is a crucial concept to grasp. The words that come out of our mouths are direct reflections of what's going on in our hearts. In short, your words are showing the world what is in your heart. If we frequently use profanity, that may be a sign that something in our hearts needs immediate adjustment.

David's prayer in Psalm 19 is for both his words and the meditation of his heart to be acceptable in God's sight. And Jesus reinforces that your speech is a reflection of your inner state. So when we hear someone say, "I love Jesus, but I cuss a little," we need to consider what that really means. While it may seem like a harmless or funny statement, it points to a deeper issue. Our words are a direct reflection of the condition of our hearts.

James 1:26 adds another layer to this discussion: "If you claim to be religious but don't control your tongue, you are fooling yourself, and your religion is worthless" (NLT). That's a pretty heavy statement. It's a reminder that our words carry more weight than we often realize. We are created in the image of God, and that means our words have power. Think about how God created the universe; He spoke it into existence. Similarly, our words have the power to shape the world around us.

Whether we realize it or not, the lives we have today are largely the result of the words we have spoken. Don't like what you see? Start by changing the way you speak. Speak life. Speak joy. Speak love. Speak peace. In Matthew 12:36–37 Jesus tells us that we will have to give an account on the day of judgment for every idle word we speak—the words we say will either acquit us or condemn us.

I think sometimes we forget that we are on a mission. In Acts 1:8 Luke recounts how Jesus gave us what is often called the "Great Commission," saying, "But you will receive power when the Holy Spirit comes upon you. And you will be my witnesses, telling people about me everywhere" (NLT). As believers this mission is central to our lives. We are called to be witnesses of Jesus, and that includes how we speak. Our words are one of the most powerful tools God has given us to carry out this mission.

When you start to see your words in the light of this mission, it changes the way you speak. You begin to ask yourself, "Is what I'm about to say going to bless this person? Is it going to build them up? Is it going to show them who Jesus really is?" If the answer is no, then why would you want to say it anyway?

Listen, my friend, Jesus isn't going to kick you out of heaven because you used a curse word. His sacrifice on the cross covered every sin, every mistake, every careless word. But the goal isn't just to make it into heaven. The goal is to become more like Jesus every day, and that includes the way we speak. God isn't mad at you for using profanity, but He does want more for you. He wants you to use your words to thank Him, to bless others, and to draw near to His presence.

So let me encourage you today.

Don't live in fear, wondering if a slip of the tongue will keep you out of heaven. Instead, focus on allowing the Holy Spirit to transform your heart so that your words reflect the new life you have in Christ. As Psalm 19:14 says, let the words of your mouth and meditation of your heart be pleasing to God. Use your words to thank God, bless others, and build them up. When you do, you will find yourself walking in the fullness of God's presence. And that's the best place you can be.

CHAPTER 4

Is It a Sin to Get a Tattoo?

THE QUESTION OF whether getting a tattoo is a sin is one that many Christians have debated over the years. It's a topic that creates divisions among believers, with some being adamant that tattoos are sinful and others feeling comfortable getting inked, especially with designs that reflect their faith. Regardless of which side you fall on, it is important to approach this question from a biblical perspective. After all, opinions are secondary to what God says through His Word.

When this topic comes up, I often hear the argument that tattoos are unequivocally sinful, with some Christians even claiming that people who have tattoos are destined for eternal damnation. No joke, while I was going through Bible college, I had a professor tell me to stand up and face the class. The professor then used me as an illustration, saying, "The only reason Kelly has these tattoos is because he allowed himself to be possessed by a demon before he got them." Can you imagine the look on my face? I was in shock!

On the flip side, other believers argue that tattoos

are harmless and not inherently sinful as long as the designs are godly or based on Scripture. Maybe you've heard these arguments as well, and it's easy to get lost in the noise. However, the problem with both positions is that they don't always bring up God's Word in their reasonings. While opinions can be interesting, they don't carry the authority that Scripture does.

So what does the Bible actually say about tattoos? Let's look and see.

The Bible does contain a specific reference to tattoos, found in Leviticus 19:28. The verse states, "You shall not make any cuttings in your flesh for the dead, nor tattoo any marks on you: I am the LORD" (NKJV). Now, at first glance it may seem that the answer is clear-cut.

But hold on a minute. There's more to consider.

If you read Leviticus 19 in its entirety, you'd notice that it also contains many other instructions, such as not trimming your beard, cutting the sides of your hair, or eating rare steak, and even the instruction to stand up whenever an elderly person with gray hair enters the room. The chapter also instructs people not to wear clothing made from mixed materials, such as cotton and polyester blends. Yet many Christians today, you and me included, don't follow *these* rules to the letter.

Why?

The truth behind Leviticus 19 and why we don't strive to follow it to a T is because these laws are part of the Old Covenant, given specifically to the Jewish people during their time in the wilderness under Moses' leadership.

The Book of Leviticus was written for the Israelites,

especially the priests, to guide them in maintaining a relationship with God during their forty-year journey through the Sinai Peninsula. These laws were designed not for the entire world but for the specific context of the Israelites' cultural and spiritual lives at that time. When we look at Leviticus 19:28 in this light, we need to ask ourselves, "Why do we focus so much on the tattoo part of this chapter while ignoring the other parts that we don't observe today?"

I'm sure you may be saying, "But wait! The law is still important, Kelly. We can't just dismiss it."

And yes, the law is important. In fact, it's vital. But let's remember what the Bible says in the New Testament about the law. Galatians 3:10 tells us, "For all who rely on the works of the law are under a curse, as it is written: 'Cursed is everyone who does not continue to do everything written in the Book of the Law.'" In other words, if you are going to say that tattoos are sinful because of the Old Testament Law, you better be prepared to follow all 613 laws outlined in the Torah! And the reality is that no one can do that. The purpose of the law is to show humanity our need for a Savior, not to be the ultimate standard for righteousness.

Thank God for Jesus Christ, who came to fulfill the law! As Christians we are no longer bound by the Old Covenant, because Jesus has ushered in a New Covenant. He has freed us from the burden of having to follow the law perfectly, something no one could ever achieve.

"OK, Kelly. Then what does Jesus say about tattoos?"

In the Gospels, the Pharisees asked Jesus which law

was the most important. Instead of responding with a lengthy list of dos and don'ts, Jesus summarized the law into two principles: "Love the Lord your God with all your heart and with all your soul and with all your mind" and "Love your neighbor as yourself" (Matt. 22:37–39). These two commandments capture the essence of the Law and the Prophets. Notice that Jesus didn't give any direct prohibitions about tattoos or external appearances in general. His focus was on love: love for God and love for others.

Some Christians may also try to show you 1 Corinthians 6:19–20 when using the New Testament in this argument. It says, "Do you not know that your bodies are temples of the Holy Spirit, who is in you, whom you have received from God? You are not your own; you were bought at a price. Therefore honor God with your bodies." This verse is often quoted in arguments against tattoos, likening them to defacing God's temple. But is that what this passage is really addressing?

In 1 Corinthians 6 Paul is specifically talking about sexual immorality. Verse 18 says, "Flee from sexual immorality. All other sins a person commits are outside the body, but whoever sins sexually, sins against their own body." The focus here is not on tattoos or external modifications to the body but rather on avoiding sexual sin, which affects not just the body but the soul and spirit as well. Tattoos, on the other hand, are purely external and do not have the same kind of impact on a person's spiritual life.

Now, at this point you may be hoping I bring up Revelation 19:16, which describes Jesus at His second coming: "On his robe and on his thigh he has this name written: KING OF KINGS AND LORD OF LORDS." Some Christians have taken this verse to mean that Jesus has a tattoo. However, interpretations vary depending on the Bible translation. Some translations suggest that the writing is on Jesus' robe, rather than His actual thigh, while others maintain that it is on His body. Either way, this passage does not provide enough concrete evidence to settle the question of whether Jesus has a tattoo, and it doesn't seem to be a key point in the overall discussion of tattoos for modern believers.

But follow me here for a minute. It's all about to become crystal clear.

In 1 Corinthians 10:23 Paul writes, "All things are lawful for me, but not all things are helpful; all things are lawful for me, but not all things edify" (NKJV). This verse is crucial when discussing tattoos. While Christians are not under the Old Testament Law, we are still called to exercise wisdom and discernment. Just because something is allowed doesn't mean it's going to benefit you. When considering whether to get a tattoo, it's important to ask yourself and the Father if it will bring honor to God for you to have it and if a tattoo aligns with the life He has called you to live.

The cultural context is also worth considering. In some cultures tattoos may be associated with negative or even sinful behaviors. In others they may be seen as art or personal expressions. As Christians we are called to be in the world but not of it, and part of that involves being mindful of how our actions are perceived by others. Will your tattoo cause someone to stumble in their faith? Or will it open doors for ministry opportunities?

Ultimately, whether to get a tattoo or not is a personal decision that each Christian must make prayerfully. The external appearance of your body, including any tattoos or piercings, does not define your relationship with God. What matters most is the condition of your heart. When you gave your life to Jesus, your spirit was made new. As a believer you are already sealed with the Holy Spirit, and nothing you put on your skin can change that.

At the end of the day your body is temporary. The Bible tells us that our flesh is sinful and will one day pass away, but our spirits will live on in eternity with God. Tattoos or piercings, or any other modifications, are all part of the body, which is perishable. However, what are eternal are your relationship with God and the condition of your soul.

So is it a sin to get a tattoo? Based on Scripture, I don't believe it is inherently sinful. But just because something is permissible doesn't mean it's the best choice for everyone.

My advice?

Pray about it. Ask God for guidance, and let the Holy Spirit lead you in making the decision that is right for you. Most importantly, remember that Jesus loves you for who you are, not for what's on your skin. He looks at your heart, your motives, and your willingness to serve Him. Whether you have tattoos or not, what matters is your commitment to living a life that honors God and reflects His love to the world.

CHAPTER 5

Does God Really Have to Test Us?

S IT NECESSARY for us to endure wilderness seasons, deserts, and storms in our spiritual journeys? Why does the Bible insist that we be tested by fire? Doesn't that seem like a bit much?

I have some really good news for you today. If you're reading this and feel as though you're going through a testing season—as if God is a million miles away and His blessings and favor seem even farther—this message is for you.

These are important questions, but most of the time, the people who ask them approach them from the wrong perspective. Their question should not be, "Do we really need to be tested by fire?" Instead, it should be, "Thank God we get to be tested by fire!" That's right. There's a profound blessing attached to this process. Think about it for a minute. Why is gold placed into fire in the first place? The purpose is to burn away all the impurities. Everything that is less than pure and less than perfect is removed in the fire, and what remains is solid, refined gold.

That's exactly what God intends to do in your life!

Many times we refer to this refining process as the desert season. Unfortunately, a lot of people view going through the desert as a form of punishment from God. But let me tell you, that couldn't be further from the truth. In reality, the desert season you may find yourself in right now is not punishment at all. It's preparation!

"Uh, OK," you say. "Preparation for what, exactly?"

It's preparation for your calling! Just as gold must be purified before it can be shaped into something beautiful, so too you must be prepared before stepping into the fullness of what God has called you to do and who He has called you to be. It may feel harsh, but it is an essential step. Now, you may be thinking, "What kind of God would allow us to go through trials and troubles just to prepare us for something?"

The answer is quite simple: one who loves you more than anything, who understands that if your character doesn't match your calling, you won't be able to sustain it. Do you see what I'm saying here? The struggles and challenges you face should be viewed as blessings, not curses. That's because the desert isn't a punishment—it's preparation for your promotion.

"Well, I wish God would hurry up with this process. I can't take much more of His testing!"

Believe me, you're not alone in feeling that way. But here's the truth: There's nothing you can do to speed up the desert season you're in. Why? Because God is working on your character, and that is something that cannot be rushed. However, there are things we can do to prolong this season, which is precisely what we don't want to do. Unfortunately, this is what happens to a lot of people. In their efforts to speed up the process, they end up making it last even longer.

Let me show you two examples, one positive and one negative. First, let's look at the Israelites. Their desert season was meant to prepare them for the Promised Land. And guess what? So is yours! This period of preparation for the Israelites was supposed to last only eleven days, but we know it took them forty years. That's right, forty years of wandering in the desert when it should have been only a brief journey. Why did this happen? First Corinthians 10 tells us exactly what went wrong. The Bible lists five things that kept the Israelites from entering their Promised Land, turning an eleven-day journey into a forty-year ordeal.

Let's take a look at this list:

1. idolatry

2. tempting God

3. lusting after evil things

4. sexual immorality

5. complaining

Did you catch that? Complaining. Pay attention here. God puts complaining on the same level as sexual immorality and idolatry! That may seem like an exaggeration, but if you ask me, the greatest sin the Israelites committed during their desert season was, indeed, complaining. And we can learn a lot from this.

Complaining keeps us stuck.

Let's not sugarcoat it. We do the exact same thing today, almost every single day. For many of us the majority of our prayers consist of telling God what we don't like about our lives. Have you ever stopped to think about that? Complaining is inherently selfish. When we complain, what we're really saying is, "I'm focused on *me* because what I want is more important than anything else."

If we're going to get real here, when you complain about the process God has you in, you're essentially saying, "God, I don't like the way You're doing things, and I think I could do them better." Whoa. That's a heavy statement, right? And it's not one you would want to say to God, is it? I didn't think so. This is why the Bible tells us to "do everything without complaining or arguing" (Phil. 2:14, bsb).

God instructs us to seek His kingdom and His righteousness, but when we spend all our time complaining, it's because we're focused on building *our* own kingdom. There's nothing wrong with bringing your concerns and situation before God, but when we constantly complain and ask Him to change our circumstances to fit our preferences, we are essentially rejecting His wisdom and His timing.

Here's the thing: God already knows what you need. He's fully aware of what you're lacking, and He knows exactly what's required for you to enter your promised land. He is trying to help, even though the process may feel uncomfortable. So if you find yourself in a desert season right now, don't get frustrated and start complaining—get excited! Start seeing it as God preparing you for your promotion!

Now, let me show you a positive example of how this process works. Remember the story of Joseph? He's the guy with the custom, one-of-a-kind, colorful coat. His story is hands down one of the best examples of how this process should unfold.

God gave Joseph a promise, a calling, a dream that was absolutely huge. (Just as the one He's given you!) But Joseph was not prepared to be a ruler at the time of God's calling. His story begins with him snitching on his brothers, and let's face it, his character at the time was not quite ready to match the magnitude of the promise. In fact, I'm pretty sure Joseph's story is where we get the phrase "snitches get stitches and wind up in ditches"! (I'm kidding! Kind of.)

What I want you to see is that Joseph had to go through a refining process. He was thrown into a pit, sold into slavery, falsely accused of a crime, and imprisoned. Yet not once did Joseph complain. The Bible tells us that he kept the promise of God at the forefront of his mind, and because he allowed his character to be developed in his desert season, everything God promised him came to pass. (See Genesis 37–50.)

Joseph could have easily become bitter and angry with God, saying, "Your promises aren't real. You're not a man of Your word. I could have done this differently." But instead, he trusted the process. Unlike the Israelites, Joseph didn't let complaints poison his progress.

Here's why complaining keeps you stuck in the wilderness. Whatever you focus on becomes the biggest thing in your life. When you're constantly complaining, your issues and struggles dominate your thoughts. They become all you can see. However, when we shift our focus back to God, we start to remember His faithfulness.

In those moments of refocusing, we say, "God, You're allowing me to go through this because You have something so much better on the other side. I trust You, Father. Whatever I need to go through, I know You're going through it with me. This is just preparation for my elevation!"

Do you see the difference in attitude? When you shift from complaining to trusting, you give God access to work in your life, and more often than not, that's when you start to see the breakthrough. It's no coincidence that when you fix your eyes on God in the middle of your wilderness, you often find yourself on the way out!

So let me encourage you today.

I may not know what specific challenges you're facing right now, but I do know this: It's all preparation for your purpose. That is a gift, not a burden. It's time to start seeing it that way.

Trust God in this process. He loves you more than anything. Don't delay the promises God has for you by allowing complaints to linger in your heart. Instead, praise Him through the process. Worship Him in the waiting. It will be 100 percent worth it in the end, and I can promise you that when you emerge from this desert season, you'll see that it was all part of His perfect plan.

After the second generation of Israelites finally entered the Promised Land, they realized that their parents' time in the wilderness had been essential. (See Deuteronomy 1:34–35.) Without it they would not have had the strength, unity, and trust in God that they needed to conquer the land. The same will be true for you. The trials and struggles you face today are setting you up for victories tomorrow. Each step, each hardship, each test is adding to your spiritual résumé, making you stronger and more capable of carrying the blessings God has in store for you.

So when the desert season feels overwhelming, when the fire feels too hot, remember that this is not the end. This is merely the preparation. God is refining you, just as gold is refined in the fire, so that you can come out stronger and purer, ready to step into the fullness of your destiny. Hold on to His promises, keep your eyes on Him, and let the process do its work. After all, the best is yet to come!

CHAPTER 6

Why Didn't God Heal My Person?

I F GOD STILL heals today, why didn't He heal *my* person?" Have you ever found yourself thinking that? Or perhaps someone has asked you that exact question in a moment of grief, confusion, or heartache. If you have ever experienced this thought or faced this question from someone else, I want to begin by telling you that you are not alone. I pray that as you read this, peace floods your heart and you find comfort, not only for your own struggles but also for the next time someone approaches you with this question, that you can help them navigate through their pain with answers from God's Word.

The realities of sickness and loss can be heart-wrenching, especially when we believe wholeheartedly in God's power to heal. In so many of my books, teachings, and social media posts, I've spoken at length about how Jesus paid for our salvation, deliverance, and healing when He gave His life on the cross. That's the truth, and it remains central to everything we believe.

That's the very first thing I want you to grab hold of today: Your healing, and the healing of those you love, have already been bought and paid for by the sacrifice of Jesus. It's crucial that this truth be ingrained in your heart, no matter what happens in the natural world around us.

Yet despite this reality, we all still witness death. We lose people we love—children, parents, spouses, and friends, and even people who were so passionate in their faith and love for God. It doesn't seem fair, and more often than not, it leaves us puzzled, asking why.

As I write this, just yesterday someone left a comment on one of my videos, expressing the pain of their loss. They mentioned how God had "taken" someone they loved from them and noted that because I seem to have so much joy all the time, I must be "lucky" that God hadn't done the same to me. Can I be completely honest with you for a moment? That comment stung, not because it was said out of malice but because the assumption was so far from the truth of what I've experienced. The truth is, I have walked through deep pain and loss, just like you may have.

Let me share something personal with you.

Two years ago I lost my stepmother, who was only fifty-five years old. Now, when I say *stepmother*, I need you to understand that Echo was never just a *step* in my life. She was simply my mom in every way that mattered. She raised me, loved me unconditionally, and was one of the most God-fearing, Christ-centered women I have ever known. Her love for Jesus was evident in everything she did, and she radiated His love to everyone around her.

When Echo started experiencing health issues, we all were concerned. She went to the doctor, who told her she had COPD. This was baffling to us all because she had never smoked a day in her life. She had never worked in environments that would have exposed her to second-hand smoke or harmful pollutants. But the doctor was insistent; COPD was the diagnosis. For three years she was treated for this condition, but as it turned out, she had been misdiagnosed. By the time they finally discovered what was truly wrong, it was too late.

Here's where my heart was at that time: I fully believed with every fiber of my being that God was going to heal her. I held on to my faith with such strength that I didn't even visit her in the hospital as often as I should have, not because I didn't care but because I was so confident that God would bring her through, heal her body, and let her walk out of that hospital with an incredible testimony. My faith was unshakable.

But guess what?

She passed away.

I'll be honest with you—I was angry. Yes, even in my faith, I experienced anger and confusion. But here's something remarkable: My faith in God hasn't changed. It didn't waver then, and it won't waver now.

You may be wondering, "How can you keep trusting God after losing your mom? How are you just OK with that?" The truth is that I wasn't OK with losing my mom. The grief was immense. But let me explain to you what God showed me in that painful season.

Just six months after my mom passed away, my grandma (who was like a second mother to me) was diagnosed with leukemia. The doctors gave her only three months to live. Once again, my family and I turned to the only thing we knew to do: We prayed, hard. We quoted Scripture, we laid hands on her, and we declared healing over her body. And just three days after her diagnosis my grandma also passed away.

Now, here's something that may sound crazy to you, especially after those two devastating losses. I'm still preaching healing in the name of Jesus. Yes, even after my mother and grandmother were not healed in the way I had prayed for, I continue to proclaim God's healing power. How can I do that? Let me tell you how.

When I was in the thick of my grief, feeling lost and confused, God revealed something powerful to me through the Scriptures. He took me to John 5, the story of Jesus healing the man at the pool of Bethesda. You may be familiar with the story, and if not, I highly recommend reading it because it's an incredible story of Jesus' compassion and miraculous power. But as I was reading it, a question burned in my mind: "Jesus, why did You heal only one man? There were so many others at the pool who needed healing. Why just him?"

Some people may say, "Well, we don't know for sure that He healed only one person; the Bible just records one healing there." While that's possible, the text does say that after Jesus healed the man, He slipped away into the crowd, because the Pharisees were looking for Him. From that context it seems unlikely that He healed anyone else that day. So I had to ask, "Why him, God? What made him so special?"

God then brought me to another passage, Acts 3. A man who couldn't walk was lying near the temple gate called the Beautiful Gate, begging for money. Peter and John approached him, and Peter famously said, "Silver and gold I do not have, but what I do have I give you: In the name of Jesus Christ of Nazareth, rise up and walk" (v. 6, NKJV). And the man got up, completely healed! The Bible goes on to tell us that over five thousand people believed in Jesus that day because of that one miracle.

Here's the critical point God showed me: This man had been lying at the temple gate every day. That means every time Jesus visited the temple complex, He had to walk right past this other man. Jesus didn't heal him then because He knew the glory that would come from his healing later, through Peter and John. The timing of that miracle was orchestrated perfectly for God's purposes.

This revelation hit me hard: God's timing is not our timing. What we often see as delay or even denial is actually God setting the stage for a greater miracle. His wisdom far exceeds ours, and His plans are beyond our understanding.

Now, I want to address another crucial point that often gets misunderstood. God doesn't take people away from us. I've heard this statement so many times—"God took my loved one." But the truth is, God doesn't take people; He receives them. He welcomes them into His eternal presence when their times on this earth come to an end. God doesn't cause tragedy or pain. He doesn't send sickness. But here's what He does do: He uses those painful moments for our good and His glory. That's why Romans 8:28 is such a powerful scripture, but it's also one of the most misquoted verses of all time.

How many times have you heard someone say, "Don't worry! God works all things for good"? It's become such a common phrase that people don't even think about the rest of the verse. But Romans 8:28 actually says, "And we know that in all things God works for the good of those who love him, who have been called according to his purpose." That's a huge difference! The verse isn't just saying that God works everything for good in a general sense. It specifically says He "works for the good of those who love him" and are "called according to his purpose." It's about His purpose, not ours.

I can't sit here and tell you exactly why God doesn't heal everyone in the ways we expect. I can't explain why one person receives an instant miracle while another suffers for years. But here's what I do know: God is good, and His love never fails. That's what the Bible says. Love never fails, and God *is* love. When we say we trust God, it doesn't mean we trust Him only when things go our way. True trust means we believe in His goodness even when we don't understand His ways. We trust Him even when the healing doesn't come the way we wanted it to.

"Yeah, but that doesn't take away the pain, Kelly."

You're right. It doesn't erase the pain. But here's another truth God reminded me of during my darkest moments: This life is temporary. The Bible says our lives are but vapors, gusts of wind that come and go (Jas. 4:14). We often get so fixated on the here and now, on the temporary pain, that we lose sight of eternity. But eternity is what truly matters.

When I cried out to God, "Why didn't You heal my mom?" He gently answered me, "I did, Kelly. She's with Me now, and she is totally healed." That realization changed everything. Healing doesn't always look the way we want it to, but that doesn't mean it didn't happen. My mom is healed. My grandma is healed. They are whole and complete and in the presence of Jesus. They received the ultimate healing.

So the question becomes, Do we trust God's plan even when it looks different from ours? Do we trust that He knows what He's doing, even when we don't? Trusting God isn't about getting the outcomes we want. It's about believing that He is working all things for good, even when we can't see it in the moment.

The truth is that you and I can't heal anyone. Only God can. But that doesn't mean we stop praying for healing. We are called to pray for healing and to trust God with the results.

I travel and preach all over the country, and I pray for people's healing almost every single day. I've seen miraculous healings happen time and time again. But not for my mom. Not for my grandma. If anyone had a reason to be bitter or angry with God, it should be me.

I've devoted my life to sharing His love and power with the world. I pray for strangers in grocery stores, gas stations, and parking lots. I've watched people get saved, healed, and set free right before my eyes. So why didn't God heal the people I love?

Here's what I realized: When we start thinking like that, we're focusing on building our kingdom instead of God's. We're telling God, "I want my life to look a certain way, and it doesn't. I'm upset with You about that." But the Bible never tells us to seek our own kingdom. It says to seek first His kingdom (Matt. 6:33). Our lives are temporary, but His kingdom is eternal. We are all dying, but Jesus conquered death. If you've given your life to Him, you've already defeated death too.

My friend, if your loved one knew Jesus and gave their life to Him, then you haven't truly lost them. You're just separated for a little while. One day you'll see them again, and that reunion will be glorious. As for me, I know that no matter what happens, I will never stop praying for healing because I trust that God is working it all for good. You know how I can be so confident? Because I love Him, and I'm called according to His purpose, not mine. His will is always better than anything I could imagine.

I know this may not be the answer you were looking for, but I hope it brings you some peace and encouragement. Never forget: God is good, and He is faithful. Keep trusting Him. Keep praying for healing until you see it. Whether it happens on this side of heaven or the other, the healing you're praying for has already been paid for by Jesus' sacrifice. When and where it manifests is in His hands. Our part is to trust.

If you're reading this and realize you've never given your life to Jesus, but you want to see your loved ones again in eternity, I have some incredible news for you. It's so simple. The Bible says that to receive the gift of salvation, all you have to do is believe in your heart that Jesus is the Son of God and confess with your mouth that He is Lord (Rom. 10:9–10). If you believe that right now, you are saved and you are in a relationship with Jesus! The next step is to live that out. You can pray right now and tell the Lord, "Today I make You the Lord of my life. I'm not building my kingdom anymore; I want to build Yours." The second way you confess He is Lord is by how you live. Every day, you seek to build His kingdom, and that kingdom will last forever.

When you get to heaven, I can't wait to meet you there. I'll bring my mom and grandma, and we'll all walk down the streets of gold together. Amen!

CHAPTER 7

Is It Wrong to Listen to Secular Music and Watch Horror Movies?

S o YOU'RE A Christian now. You gave your life to Jesus, and you've been spending time in His Word. But what about the music you listen to? What about the movies you watch? Does that stuff have to change now that you are a follower of Jesus? As believers do we only listen to worship? Do we watch movies and TV shows only about Jesus?

Those are some really good and very honest questions. And if you've been wondering about these things, you're not alone. So let's walk through this together and see what the Bible says.

Right out of the gate the Bible does tell us that our walk of God is a journey. It also says, in so many words, "Don't stop believing." And those aren't out of the "Book of Steve Perry"!

Look, I can show you a million scriptures on how important it is to be intentional about what we put in our minds, because what we think about, we will speak about. And Proverbs 18:21 says that death and life rest in the power of the tongue. Are you catching the weight of this?

Genesis 1:26 starts with God saying, "Let us make human beings in our image, to be like us" (NLT). Let me ask you a question. Whose image were you created in? God's! And how does God create *anything*? He speaks! The same goes for you and me, since He created us in His image.

You have to understand that your words are one of the most powerful tools you have. You're creating the world around you every time you speak, and you're speaking about what you put in it! This is why the Bible also tells us that we are defiled not by what goes *in* us but rather by what comes *out* of us (Matt. 15:11). What you put in your mind, you will think about. What you think about, you will speak about. And what you speak about, you will see more of in your life because you are creating every time you speak!

No verse in the Bible is going to tell you, "Listen to only Hillsong and Elevation Worship." It doesn't say, "You can watch only *The Chosen* and *Fireproof*." As a Christian you can still do anything you want. You have free will. But there's one scripture, only one, that you really need to know when asking this question: Ephesians 4:30, which says, "Do not bring sorrow to God's Holy Spirit by the way you live. Remember, he has identified you as his own, guaranteeing that you will be saved on the day of redemption" (NLT).

Oh son! Did you catch that?

What that verse just told us is that when you got saved, you got a new roommate—the Holy Spirit! And have you ever had a roommate before? Yeah, I'm sure you're being flooded with amazing memories right now, aren't you? The fact is, when you start sharing your life with another person, things have to change. You can't live life the way you did before. Right? I can't just walk around the living room in my underwear at 10 a.m. anymore. I might bring *sorrow* to someone! Are you following me here? You adjust the way you live because of who's living with you. And the thing about the roommates I've had in my life is that if we ever stopped getting along, or if they did something I didn't like, no big deal. I'm out! I'd go find a new place to live, with somebody else.

But that's not how God works. See, my Bible says He will *never* leave you or forsake you (Deut. 31:6; Heb. 13:5). So that means when we get saved and the Holy Spirit starts living on the inside of us, He's not going to leave us, regardless of what we do.

"OK, Kelly. So you're saying the Holy Spirit lives in me. He's my roommate, and He's not ever leaving. What does that have to do with listening to secular music or watching movies?"

Great question. I'm so glad you asked.

We love to say that Jesus lives in our hearts, but that's not actually true. Jesus is at the right hand of the Father, interceding on your behalf (Rom. 8:34). The Holy Spirit is who we have on this earth. And since He chooses to live in you, that means He goes where you go. He watches what you watch. He listens to what you listen to. Now, stop and think for a minute. When was the last time you even considered the Holy Spirit? When was the last time you asked Him, "Do You want to watch this? Do You want to listen to this? Do You want to go here?"

So many people have the Holy Spirit as their roommate, yet they hardly ever communicate with Him, let alone ask Him what He would like to do. How ridiculous would it be if I came to visit you, and if everywhere you went, I went. You're in the car; I'm in the car, sitting next to you. You go eat; I go eat. But I never say a word to you. I'm there with you in all things, but just silent. Then, at the end of the week, before I go home, I finally speak up. "Hey, friend, I'm really hurting on my rent this month. I don't know if I can pay it. Do you think you could help me out a little bit?"

Ouch.

You mean you want to talk to me only when you need something? Sound familiar? So many people have the Holy Spirit in them, and yet they never acknowledge Him.

This is why Ephesians 4:30 says, "Do not bring sorrow to God's Holy Spirit by the way you live." Please understand—you don't have to ask me or anyone else, "Is this a sin? Is that a sin? Can I do this as a Christian? Will I go to heaven if I do this?" Don't you know God lives in you? Ask Him! He'll tell you what He wants to do. He'll let you know if He doesn't want to watch it. He'll let you know if He doesn't want to listen to it. But you have to ask!

I'll be real with you. I don't listen to *just* Christian

music, but I *always* listen to the Holy Spirit. If I get in my car and turn on The Pixies, and if the Holy Spirit tells me, "Kelly, I don't want to listen to The Pixies. Let's worship together!" I don't play The Pixies, because I'd rather please Him than please my flesh. Not to mention, when you pair the revelation of the Holy Spirit being your roommate with the revelation of how powerful your words are, it makes for a pretty easy choice.

Let me show you how this should work in real life.

Should I watch a horror movie? Well, I know that what I put in my mind, I will think about, speak about, and see more of in my life. And what is the purpose of a horror movie? To incite fear. But my Bible tells me in 2 Timothy 1:7 that God has given us a spirit not of fear but of power and of love and of a sound mind. Fear is *not* from the Lord! So why would I want to bring that into my life?

"I get that, Kelly. But I'm not afraid when I watch movies like that. It's just a form of entertainment."

OK, fair enough.

So let's move on to step 2 in this process. If you feel that whatever it is you want to watch or listen to is just fine for you, now it's time to ask your roommate, "Holy Spirit, would You like to watch this horror movie?" I'm not going to lie—I laughed while writing that line, because some questions don't even need to be asked. Sometimes we can't hear God speak when we ask a question, because He doesn't need to. He already wrote the answer to you in His Word!

Nevertheless, let's keep going. So now you have asked

the Holy Spirit if He wants to watch a particular movie. But what if you aren't hearing an answer? Well, like I said before, it could be that you already *know* the answer in your heart. You *know* the Holy Spirit doesn't want to watch all that violence, filthy language, and lust. So don't do it! We can make this process way harder than it needs to be sometimes.

But let's say it's not so easy to see.

"What if I just want to listen to Journey? There's no filthy language in those songs. They aren't bad in comparison with everything else out there I could be listening to. I've asked the Holy Spirit if He wants to listen to this, but now I'm trying to back out of my driveway, I'm late for work, and I'm not hearing an answer."

God will always lead you with peace. The enemy will push you and pull you with stress, anxiety, fear, and depression. If you're backing out of your driveway, about to jam to some music from your childhood, and don't have a peace about listening to it—or, alternatively, watching it, doing it, going there, whatever—don't do it! Stress and anxiety are not from God. If you don't have a peace about it (whatever *it* may be), that's your answer.

So let me encourage you today.

Your words are powerful. Be mindful of what you let in your mind, because it's going to get in your heart and pour out your mouth. And whether you like it or not, your mouth is shaping the world around you. Most of all, my friend, never forget you have the most amazing and wonderful roommate of all time living inside you. Don't bring sorrow to Him by the way you live. He wants to spend time with you. So spend time with Him. Ask Him what He would like to do today. And if you have a peace about it, don't let anyone steal that from you. Keep a smile on your face, knowing that if your roommate is pleased with you, that's all that really matters anyway!

CHAPTER 8

Is It a Sin to Use Marijuana?

HIS IS A question I hear often, and it's one of those questions that never seem to go away. But before we dive into it, let me express something right off the bat: I'm not a fan of the question "Is it a sin?" We've discussed this question a few times already, and my concern is that the question itself can be limiting. You see, I get asked questions like this multiple times a day, and what I hope you are learning as you walk through this book with me is that our focus should not be always on whether something is labeled as a sin. Instead, the focus should be on cultivating a relationship with the Holy Spirit, who resides within us as believers. The Spirit of God is our personal Guide, Counselor, and Teacher, and we can rely on Him to lead us into truth. So rather than asking others, "Is this a sin in my life?" we should learn to ask the Holy Spirit directly. He knows us intimately and desires to guide us.

However, for the sake of this discussion, let's take a closer look at what the Bible says about the topics of sin and personal responsibility and at how we approach the question of marijuana use, in light of God's Word.

First, we need to establish a clear understanding of what sin really is. This is crucial because without this understanding, we may struggle with identifying whether certain actions or behaviors are sinful in our lives. The Bible defines sin as anything that separates us from God or anything we place above God in our lives. Essentially, it's putting something in the place that belongs only to Him.

In the most basic terms, sin is idolatry. It's choosing something or someone over God, whether it's a behavior, a thought pattern, or a dependency, on anything, that takes precedence over your relationship with God. So the key question we must ask ourselves when discussing marijuana is, "Am I using marijuana as a form of fulfillment in my life?" If the answer to that question is yes, then we are placing marijuana in a position that should belong only to God, and that's where the issue of sin comes into play.

When we seek fulfillment in things such as drugs or alcohol, work, relationships, or entertainment, we're essentially saying, "These will bring me the peace and satisfaction I desire." The problem with this is that only Jesus can truly satisfy the deep longings of our hearts. When we turn to anything else for fulfillment, we end up feeling empty over and over again because nothing in this world can bring the peace, joy, and lasting fulfillment Jesus offers.

The truth is, we all have a natural inclination to run

to something or someone when we're seeking comfort, peace, or relief from the stresses of life. For some it's drugs. For others it may be money or relationships, or even work. The issue arises when those things take the place of God in our lives. If you're using marijuana as a crutch to deal with stress or anxiety or to find peace, then clearly, it has become a substitute for what only God can provide. In that case yes, it's wrong. It's that simple.

Now, I often hear people argue, "But what if I'm using marijuana for medical reasons? It's been prescribed by a doctor." I understand that argument, and I don't discount the legitimate medical uses for marijuana, especially when it comes to managing chronic pain or other medical conditions. However, my response to this question is always the same: Have you first sought God in those areas of your life?

We are so blessed to live in a time when medical advancements have given us incredible resources and medications to help manage physical and emotional pain. I believe God has given us doctors and medicine as tools for healing and comfort. I also believe that God can and does work through these means, including marijuana when used for medical purposes. But—and this is an important *but*—God always desires to be the first place we turn to for help.

When you are in pain or dealing with anxiety, have you brought your needs before God? Have you invited Him into those areas of your life and asked for His healing and comfort? The Bible teaches us to seek first the kingdom of God, and that means bringing our burdens, our pain, and our anxieties to Him, before we turn to other sources. If we've done that, and if we feel peace about using marijuana for medical reasons, alongside seeking God's presence daily, then I believe there is nothing inherently wrong it.

Remember that God is more concerned with the *why* behind our actions than the *what*. It's not necessarily about the substance itself; it's about your heart posture. James 4:17 says, "If anyone, then, knows the good they ought to do and doesn't do it, it is sin for them." In other words, if you've truly sought God on this matter and feel no conviction, and if using marijuana is not taking the place of God in your life, you are likely in the clear. The key thing to remember is to always follow His peace.

This brings us to another important aspect of this discussion—the legality of marijuana. Some states and nations have legalized marijuana for medical purposes, and others have legalized it for recreational use as well. But what does the Bible say about following the laws of the land? In Romans 13:1–2 we're instructed to submit to governing authorities because all authority has been established by God. This means we are to respect the laws of our governments, as long as those laws don't contradict God's Word.

If marijuana is legal in your state or nation, and if you are using it in accordance with the law, then this teaching applies to you. However, if you live in a place where marijuana is illegal, and if you choose to use it anyway, you are in violation of the law, and according to Romans 13, this is not honoring to God. We don't get to pick and choose which laws we follow based on our personal preferences. God's Word calls us to submit to the laws of the land, and that includes drug laws. I understand this may not be a popular opinion, but it's what the Bible teaches. If your state or nation has not legalized marijuana and you are using it illegally, you are in the wrong, no matter what your reasoning may be.

Now, let's address the issue of recreational marijuana use. You may be living in a place where marijuana is legal for both medical and recreational use, and you may wonder, "Is it OK for me to use marijuana recreationally?" The Bible doesn't explicitly mention marijuana, but it does give us some principles to live by that can help guide our decision-making.

Again, just as we did in our discussion over tattoos, let's go to 1 Corinthians 10:23. Paul wrote, "All things are lawful for me, but not all things are helpful; all things are lawful for me, but not all things edify" (NKJV). Just because something is legal doesn't mean it's beneficial for your spiritual walk. The question you need to ask yourself is, "Why am I doing this?" If you're using marijuana recreationally, what is your motivation? Is it to escape reality, to feel a certain way, or to fill a void in your life? If so, that's a sign it's taking the place of God in your life.

Additionally, the Bible calls us to be sober minded (1 Pet. 5:8). While the passage isn't talking specifically about marijuana or even alcohol, the principle still applies. Being sober minded means being in control of your thoughts and actions, being alert, and not allowing anything to cloud your judgment or distort your reality. It's difficult to be sober minded when you're under the influence of a mind-altering substance, whether that's marijuana, alcohol, or any other drug.

When we talk about sin, it's important to understand that not all sin leads to the same consequences. If I say that using marijuana inappropriately is a sin, I'm not saying, "You're going to hell." This type of sin is no different from other sins we commit in our daily lives. It's not the same as rejecting Jesus as Lord but rather is an indication that you may not yet have fully understood or received the revelation of who God is and the fulfillment He offers.

The Christian walk is a journey, and none of us have it all figured out overnight. God knows that too, and He offers us grace along the way. My encouragement to you is get as close to Jesus as you can and allow Him to work in your heart. As you draw closer to Him, your views and opinions on worldly things will begin to change. The things that once brought you fulfillment will no longer satisfy, because you will have experienced the true fulfillment that comes from a deep relationship with Jesus.

At the end of the day, every decision we make should be filtered through the question "Is this bringing me closer to God or taking me further away from Him?" There is no neutral ground. Either the things we engage in are drawing us closer to Jesus, or they are pulling us further from Him.

So whether it's marijuana or anything else in life, always ask yourself why you're doing what you're doing.

Is it leading you into a deeper relationship with God? Is it helping others see Jesus in you? Or is it something that's pulling you away from Him? These are the questions that matter most.

So let me encourage you today!

It's not about what you do; it's about *why* you do it. Stay close to Jesus; let Him love you right where you are, but also be open to the fact that He may not want to leave you where you are. Follow Him, trust Him, and allow Him to make the necessary changes in your life. I promise you, He will never ask you to give up something without offering you something far better in return.

CHAPTER 9

Can Christians Live
Together Before Marriage?

SHOULD A CHRISTIAN couple live together before getting married? Oh son! I hope you're wearing your steel-toed boots while reading this one. I may not have the answer you're hoping for, but I will show you what the Bible says!

I've heard a lot of people say, "The Bible doesn't actually talk about this subject. So that must mean it's totally fine, right?" Let me just be honest; the Bible doesn't mention *not doing meth* either. But I mean, come on. We know better, right? The Bible doesn't come right out and plainly say a lot of things, but that doesn't mean the answer isn't there.

So what does the Bible say about living together before marriage? Well, in Matthew 19:5 Jesus explains, "A man leaves his father and mother and is joined to his wife, and the two are united into one" (NLT). Did you catch that? It says the man leaves his parents and "is joined to his wife." Not his girlfriend, not his fiancée, not some girl he really likes—*his wife*.

Now, I understand that times have changed and that we live in a different culture and day and age. But the principle remains the same. We don't typically live with our parents until we get married these days. That was an older custom that has been a bit lost on us. The point is, when we are ready to move on to the next step in life, from being alone to being in a committed relationship, we don't leave singleness until we are married. Today, "leaving your parents" would be the equivalent of moving out of your own place and moving into a new one with your wife or husband. There is a clear picture here that when the couple does start living together, they are married! Our culture today says, "That's ridiculous. Try it out first! Make sure you're compatible! Make sure it works!" But let me tell you the truth: That's what dating is for. And you don't have to live together to find out those things.

I know what you may be thinking. "Well, you know, for us it just makes sense. It's too expensive for us each to have our own place while we're trying to save for a wedding." OK, I feel you, and that seems like a legitimate reason to go ahead and move in together. After all, we do want to be wise with our finances! But let me run this thought by you: What you're really saying, whether you even realize it or not, is that you, not God, are the provider, that God is big, but not big enough to help you financially while you're honoring His Word.

Ouch.

Listen, God cares way more about you honoring Him and making choices that honor His Word than about the cost of you both having rent to pay. God is your provider. Not you. Not your job. Not your parents. And when you honor Him and His Word, He will honor you (1 Sam. 2:30). He will bless you for that! Yes, it may be difficult for a season. Yes, you may have to make adjustments. But wouldn't it be better to go into one of the biggest decisions of your life with God's full blessing and favor on you than without? Seems like a pretty easy choice to me.

Not long ago I was going to officiate a wedding for a couple who went to my church. A few months after agreeing to do the ceremony, I heard that they had moved in with each other. So I called them and asked them to come meet with me. I wanted to understand the reason for their decision because I knew they both loved the Lord and wanted to enter into a *blessed* marriage. So when I asked why they had made the choice to move in together before the wedding, their reply caught me off guard. They said they felt as if God had told them it was OK for them to live together. They said they weren't sleeping together and could withstand the temptation. Immediately, I said, "Well, that's awesome you're able to do that. I know I couldn't. I mean, my wife is hot! Temptation would get me every time." But the next question I asked changed everything.

"And what scripture are you standing on as the foundation for what God told you?"

Crickets.

You see, God will never speak something to you that contradicts His written Word, meaning He will never tell you it's OK for you to do something His Word says not to. If God speaks it to you, you should have multiple scriptures to stand on to back up what He spoke to you. If you don't, that wasn't from God!

The devil is crafty. He knows the Bible better than you or I ever will. And he's had thousands of years of practice to perfect sounding like God when he lies to you. He is extremely good at his job, and he knows exactly what to say to make you think it's God speaking to you when in reality it's not. This is why the Bible tells us to take every thought captive and "make it obedient to Christ" (2 Cor. 10:5). You have to run everything through the Word of God.

Now, can you live together before you're married and still be saved and get into heaven? Yes! You absolutely can. And God isn't mad or angry with you because of it. Jesus paid the price for you. You have freedom in Christ. You can live together before you get married if you want to. But what most people never take time to consider is, "What am I missing out on by making this choice?" You see, God isn't mad at you; He's sad. Our God is a good Father, and He wants to bless us and give good gifts to His children. But just like when my kids disobey my word, I'm disappointed. I don't love them any less, but now they may miss out on something amazing I wanted to give them or do for them if they had just obeyed me.

This making sense?

When we make choices that go against God's Word, we sacrifice a blessing, gift, promotion, healing, or break-through we could have received if we had chosen to obey instead. Marriage is hard—possibly one of the most difficult things we can go through in this life. But it's also one of the most rewarding. If it were up to me, I would want to go into something as big as marriage with God's hand of favor, blessing, and protection on me.

God loves marriage. He created it! But we can't forget that He is also a God of order. If you follow His plan and leave your singleness situation to be joined to your husband or wife, you will have followed that order. And He absolutely will bless your marriage. Will your marriage be cursed, then, if you do it the wrong way? No! He is still a good Father. There is grace. But it won't be the same. You may have to go through some difficult times that could have been avoided, not because God is mad but rather because you chose to do it your own way instead.

This brings up another question, though, doesn't it? "What if we are already living together, and now we see that we have made a mistake? How do we get back to God's favor, blessing, and protection?" And that is an excellent question! If you are reading this right now and realize you have done this wrong, I have some great news for you! Not only does God have grace for you in this area, but He also gave you a gift that will help you get right back to where you want to be.

"And what is that gift?" you ask.

Repentance!

Please understand, Jesus already paid the price for your mistake, on the cross two thousand years ago. Your mistake has already been paid for, forgiven, and forgotten by our Father. Now, sin does separate us from the Father, His blessings, His favor, His protection, His everything. But repentance puts us right back! That's why repentance is a gift. So if you realize you need to make this right with God, all you have to do is change your mind (and if you are asking this question, clearly you have) and change your direction. Now that you think differently about living together before marriage, make a change. If you aren't married but are living together currently, perhaps one of you needs to start staying with a friend or family member until the wedding. Or just go get married! Seriously, it's not that hard to find a way to honor the Lord. We are the ones who make it difficult, not Him.

And if you are already married but lived together first and now want to make things right, you can! Remember, God is looking at your heart. If you have truly made a mind change and a heart change, God sees that. Just take some time today to let Him know, "I'm sorry I didn't honor Your Word before I got married. But I see now that You had a better plan for my life. Thank You for forgiving me. I put my trust in You today." Do you see how easy that is? Repentance is truly one of the greatest gifts God ever gave us.

So let me encourage you today.

Don't live in fear of God punishing you if you have been or plan on living with your person before you get married. He's not some mean old man in the sky just waiting for you to make a mistake so He can punish you. He *loves* you! And He wants to bless you! The key to it all is understanding that the blessing is always attached to honoring His Word.

Whatever you choose to do—and this goes for any decision you make in life—make sure you have scriptures to stand on to back up your decision. (Personally, anytime I think I hear God speak to me, I instantly ask that He would show me three scriptures that align with what I just heard.) And if you don't, well, maybe you need to rethink that decision. I promise you that whatever you choose to do in this life, it will be way better to honor God's Word and go into it with His blessing than to try to do it on your own without it.

CHAPTER 10

Do We Have to Go to Church?

THE QUESTION OF whether Christians have to attend church or if it's enough to maintain a private relationship with God has been debated many times. I've heard some say, "You better be in church, or you're going to hell. God commands it!" Yet others I've heard argue, "I don't go to church at all. Those pastors just want my money. Churches are full of hypocrites. I can have a relationship with God without ever setting foot in a church building."

While these arguments are familiar to us, it's important to ask, "What does the Bible actually say about the necessity of going to church?"

Let's start by looking at Hebrews 10:24–25: "Let us consider how we may spur one another on toward love and good deeds, not giving up meeting together, as some are in the habit of doing, but encouraging one another—and all the more as you see the Day approaching." This verse, which some interpret as a call to attend church regularly, encourages Christians to meet together and not neglect gathering. However, others may argue that this verse doesn't explicitly refer to going to a church building.

It is important to note that the church is not just a *building*. The Bible often refers to us Christians as the *church*—meaning the people, not the structure. However, the passage from Hebrews emphasizes the importance of meeting together. The real question we need to ask here is, Do you truly feel as if this command doesn't apply to you? I mean, if you believe that God's Word applies to everyone else but you, it may be time to reconsider your belief!

I've also heard many people say, "I would go to church if I could find the perfect one." To this my response is simple: "If you found the perfect church, you'd ruin it by joining!" There is no such thing as a perfect church. It doesn't exist. Why? Because churches are made up of imperfect people. This speaks to an important issue many face regarding church attendance—the idea that church should cater to our personal preferences and that if it doesn't, it's not worth attending.

One common complaint is that "there are too many hypocrites in church." But let's think about this for a second. Hypocrisy exists everywhere, whether in a church, a bar, or any social setting. Yet this criticism seems to be reserved almost exclusively for churches. Why do we hold churches to a different standard? Everyone, to some degree, struggles with hypocrisy. It's part of the human condition known as the flesh.

The process of sanctification—the spiritual journey of becoming more like Christ—won't be completed for *anyone* until Jesus returns or we go to heaven. Being part of a church community means accepting that we are all in different stages of this process. Making mistakes or sinning doesn't necessarily make someone a hypocrite; it just means they're still growing in their faith.

The Bible says not to neglect meeting together. Do you have to attend a church service in a formal setting to honor God's Word? No! Not at all. But it's worth considering what you're missing out on if you don't. If you're part of a small group that meets in homes or coffee shops, or any other setting, to discuss faith, encourage one another, and grow spiritually, that's great! Don't stop doing that. However, for those who aren't involved in any kind of regular gathering, there's a risk of falling into deception.

Let me explain.

The devil works hard to isolate believers. He wants you all alone. One of his strategies is convincing people they don't need church. He loves to suggest, "You can have a relationship with God without going to church." But the Bible teaches the exact opposite. When believers isolate themselves, they become easier targets for spiritual attacks. Like predators who target prey that is alone or weak, the enemy seeks to isolate Christians from the safety and support of community. Isolation makes you vulnerable, while community helps protect and strengthen you in your faith.

Being surrounded by a group of like-minded believers helps with and encourages spiritual growth, accountability, and support. When you're involved in a church, you're consistently exposed to teaching, worship, and fellowship that build you up and make you less vulnerable to the enemy's attacks. Yes, it's possible to have a relationship with God without attending church. But by doing so, you miss out on the *amazing* blessings that come from being part of a community.

One of those blessings is the opportunity to be sharpened by others. Proverbs 27:17 says, "As iron sharpens iron, so one person sharpens another." This sharpening occurs in community, where believers can help one another grow through encouragement, correction, and prayer. When you avoid church, you miss out on the wisdom and insight that other Christians bring into your life. You didn't think only the pastor could do that, did you? Not to mention, there are blessings *you* may be called to share with others. Sometimes God works through you to bless someone else. Your presence at church may make a difference in someone else's life. If you don't go, they don't get blessed!

Here is another comment I've heard that is worth mentioning: "I don't like what my pastor says or how he preaches, so I don't think I'm going to go anymore."

Facepalm.

My friend, we have to remember that pastors, just like everyone else, are flawed individuals. As a pastor myself, I have no issue with telling you we make mistakes. We're on the same journey of faith as the rest. While pastors hold leadership roles, they still need grace just as much as anyone else.

The real question here is, Are you attending church only for what you can get for yourself?

For far too many people, church is seen as a place to consume spiritual teachings and receive blessings. That means when the pastor's message doesn't resonate with them, or when the worship doesn't include their favorite songs, they start looking for another church or even stop attending altogether. This mindset is what some would call that of a *spiritual consumer*. It's focused on what we can receive rather than what we can give. But church is not just about receiving. It's also about contributing.

If you switch your perspective to that of a *spiritual contributor*, church will become less about what you can get out of it and more about what you can offer to others. Perhaps there's someone at church who needs to hear your story, receive your encouragement, or be uplifted by your faith. There could be people whose lives are transformed just by interacting with *you* at church. God may use you as a vessel to bless someone else. But this can happen only if you're present and engaged in a church community.

Consider the analogy of the Sea of Galilee and the Dead Sea. Both bodies of water are fed by the Jordan River, but the Sea of Galilee is full of life. Why? Because it has both an inflow and an outflow. In contrast, the Dead Sea is, well, dead. Why? Because it has only an inflow and no outflow. This serves as a spiritual metaphor. If you are constantly taking in spiritual knowledge, teachings, and blessings without sharing them or serving others, you, as well, can become spiritually stagnant, just like the Dead Sea. Church gives you the opportunity to receive (inflow) and give (outflow), creating a healthy balance in your spiritual life.

So let me ask you, Why aren't you going to church? Is it because you feel the sermons don't speak to you, the people seem unfriendly, or you're just too busy? Whatever the reason, it's important to examine it honestly before God. If this book isn't convincing enough on its own, ask Him what He wants for you. The Bible makes it clear that Christians are meant to gather together, whether in church settings or smaller groups. At the end of the day we need the encouragement, accountability, and teachings that come from a community. And don't forget, there are people who need the gifts, wisdom, and encouragement that you bring as well.

Attending church isn't about checking off a box on a religious to-do list. It's about being part of a body of believers who support and strengthen one another in their walk with God. Yes, there are challenges in any church. But the benefits of being in a community far outweigh the drawbacks.

When you actively participate in church, you're not just receiving; you're contributing to the growth and well-being of others. You're helping build *His* kingdom, which is the true purpose of the church. Jesus called us to love and serve one another, and being part of a church is one way to live out that calling.

In conclusion, do Christians *have* to go to church? Strictly speaking, no, they don't. But why wouldn't you want to? The benefits of community, encouragement, spiritual growth, and opportunities to serve others are tremendous. Church is a place where you can be equipped, encouraged, and challenged to live out your faith more fully. And who knows, you may be the person God uses to change someone else's life!

CHAPTER 11

Once Saved, Always Saved?

THE QUESTION OF "once saved, always saved?" is one of the most divisive and, in some ways, dangerous topics for believers after they give their lives to Jesus. It's a question that directly impacts how we walk out our relationship with Him. This concept, of whether salvation is eternally secure or can be lost, touches the core of how we live our lives as Christians. Let's dive into this critical issue and explore what the Bible says.

The debate over whether the Bible teaches once saved, always saved, or whether it's possible to lose salvation, has been ongoing for centuries. People on both sides of the argument present compelling biblical evidence. Some point to verses like John 10:28, where Jesus says, "I give them eternal life, and they shall never perish; no one will snatch them out of my hand." Others quote scriptures such as Hebrews 6:4–6, which suggests that those who have been enlightened and then fall away cannot be brought back to repentance.

Both arguments are rooted in Scripture, making the discussion even more complex. But the real question we need to ask ourselves is, "What is the true teaching of the Bible?" Let's start by examining one of the most frequently cited scriptures in support of once saved, always saved.

John 10:28–29 is often presented as the strongest evidence for eternal security in salvation. Jesus says, "I give them eternal life, and they shall never perish; no one will snatch them out of my hand. My Father, who has given them to me, is greater than all; no one can snatch them out of my Father's hand." At face value this seems to affirm that once someone is saved, their salvation is eternally secure. After all, Jesus assures us that no one can take away those whom the Father has given Him.

However, we can't simply isolate one verse and make it the foundation for our entire theological perspective. Context is crucial when interpreting any scripture. To fully grasp what Jesus is teaching here, we need to consider the surrounding verses and the broader message of John 10.

In John 10 Jesus is speaking to a group of religious people who are questioning His identity. These were individuals who believed in God, and many of them would have considered themselves faithful followers of Him. In today's context we might say they were "religious" or "churchgoers." Jesus tells them, "I did tell you, but you do not believe. The works I do in my Father's name testify about me, but you do not believe because you are not my sheep" (vv. 25–26).

Notice that Jesus distinguishes between those who claim to believe and those who are truly His sheep. He says, "My sheep listen to my voice; I know them, and they follow me" (v. 27). This is a key point. Those who are truly saved (Jesus' sheep) are not people who merely claim to believe in Him; they are people who listen to His voice and follow His teachings. Their lives reflect their faith through their actions.

When Jesus says that no one can snatch His sheep from His hand, He is referring to those who are actively following Him. *Following* someone implies action. It means walking where they walk, doing what they do, and adhering to their guidance. In the context of John 10, those who are saved are those who continue to follow Jesus, listen to His voice, and live in obedience to His commands.

The implication here is that salvation is not just about a onetime confession of faith. It's about an ongoing relationship with Jesus, marked by obedience and discipleship. This raises a crucial question: If someone stops following Jesus, are they still His sheep?

You may be thinking right now, "But the Bible says we are saved by faith, not by works." And that is absolutely true. Ephesians 2:8–9 reminds us, "For it is by grace you have been saved, through faith—and this is not from yourselves, it is the gift of God—not by works, so that no one can boast." Our salvation is indeed a gift from God, received through faith alone.

However, true faith produces action. James 2:17 tells us, "Faith by itself, if it is not accompanied by action, is dead." If someone claims to believe in Jesus but continues to live in a way that is completely contrary to His teachings, we have to ask, "Is their faith genuine?"

Imagine a person who says they *believe* that touching a live power line will electrocute them. If they truly believe that, they will avoid touching the power line. But if they walk over and grab the power line anyway, their actions show that they don't really believe what they claim.

In the same way, Jesus says, "By their fruit you will recognize them" (Matt. 7:16). The *fruit* Jesus refers to is the actions and attitudes that come from a transformed life. If someone truly believes in Jesus, their life will show it. They will bear fruit that aligns with the teachings of Jesus.

One of the key arguments against once saved, always saved comes from scriptures that speak of people who fall away from the faith. Hebrews 6:4–6 warns about those who have been enlightened, tasted the heavenly gift, shared in and with the Holy Spirit, and then fallen away. The passage suggests that it is impossible for such individuals to be brought back to repentance.

So can a believer lose their salvation?

It's important to clarify that salvation is not something like a set of car keys that we lose. It's not something that slips away from us due to carelessness or a single mistake. However, it is possible to turn away from God deliberately and reject the gift of salvation that was once received.

When someone gives their life to Jesus, they are entering into a covenant relationship with Him. Like any relationship, this requires commitment and faithfulness. If someone decides they no longer want to follow Jesus and returns to a life of sin without repentance, they are essentially walking away from that relationship.

Salvation is not a onetime event. It's a lifelong journey. The Bible describes the Christian life as a race (Heb. 12:1) and as a battle (Eph. 6:10–18). These metaphors suggest that following Jesus requires perseverance, effort, and ongoing commitment. Paul wrote in Philippians 2:12, "Continue to work out your salvation with fear and trembling." This doesn't mean we earn our salvation, but it does mean we take it seriously and actively pursue a closer relationship with Jesus.

Those who are saved will persevere in their faith. They will continue to follow Jesus, repent when they sin, and seek to live in obedience to His Word. But those who claim to be saved but have no desire to follow Jesus or live according to His teachings may need to examine whether their faith is genuine.

The danger in the once saved, always saved doctrine lies in the potential for complacency. If someone believes they can just say a prayer, claim to believe in Jesus, and then go on living however they want, they are deceiving themselves. As James 2:19 points out, "Even the demons believe—and shudder!" (ESV). Belief alone, without a life of action that reflects that belief...

Well, actions speak louder than words, my friend.

True salvation is marked by transformation. When we give our lives to Jesus, we are "born again" (John 3:3). This means our old way of living dies, and we begin a new life in Christ. It's not just about believing the right things; it's about living in a way that reflects that belief.

So what should we take away from all this? First, we don't need to live in constant fear of losing our salvation. If you've repented of your sin, have given your life to Jesus, and are following Him closely, you are secure in your salvation. Jesus promises that no one can snatch you from His hand if you are truly His.

At the same time, we need to be cautious about complacency. Salvation is not a license to live however we want. It's a call to follow Jesus, to live in obedience to His teachings, and to be transformed by His grace. A true believer's actions will align with their words. As 1 John 2:6 says, "Whoever claims to live in him must live as Jesus did."

Let this be an encouragement to draw closer to Jesus every day. As you follow Him, you will experience the assurance of your salvation, not because of a doctrine or belief but because of the ongoing relationship you have with your Savior.

CHAPTER 12

Should Christians Celebrate Christmas and Halloween?

CHRISTIANS AND HOLIDAYS. It seems this can be a more controversial topic than whether *Die Hard* is a Christmas movie! (It is!) As followers of Jesus, should we still celebrate holidays such as Christmas and Halloween? Or do we avoid them like the plague? Let's look at both and see what the Bible says.

Starting with Christmas, I'm sure you've heard all the same arguments I've heard against Christians celebrating this holiday: "The Bible *clearly* says not to have a Christmas tree in your house!" "Christmas is a pagan holiday. We don't allow that garbage in our house!" "Telling your kids there's a Santa Claus is a lie. You want them to grow up thinking Jesus is a lie too?"

Does the Bible say we shouldn't have Christmas trees in our homes? The verses that this argument is taken from are in Jeremiah 10:1–5. In the New Living Translation, this chapter starts with the heading "Idolatry Brings Destruction." Then it goes on to say, "Do not act like the other nations....They cut down a tree, and a craftsman carves an idol. They decorate it with gold and silver and then fasten it securely with hammer and nails so it won't fall over" (vv. 2–4, NLT).

"Well, there ya have it! A tree with silver and gold? Don't be like them? That answers it right there. Christmas trees are *evil*."

Now, hold on there, Bible-thumper. When was the last time you *carved* your Christmas tree? "Uh, never." That's because this isn't talking about Christmas trees. These verses are talking about making wooden idols and worshipping them as gods. Are you worshipping and praying to your Christmas tree? If not, this isn't talking to you!

Please understand there is no verse in the Bible that tells you not to have a Christmas tree. This passage has been taken out of context, and people want to use it to defend their own ideas about Christmas when in reality these verses are about the worship of idols, not about Christmas trees.

"OK, but still, Christmas is a pagan holiday, and we should stay away from it." All right, I see where you're coming from. But let me show you something else. Colossians 2:16–17, under the heading "Freedom from Human Rules" (NIV), says, "Therefore do not let anyone judge you by what you eat or drink, or with regard to a religious festival, a New Moon celebration or a Sabbath day. These are a shadow of the things that were to come; the reality, however, is found in Christ." This is saying to not worry about what people think of you. Eat what you want, and celebrate whichever holidays and festivals you want, because Jesus changed everything. Why do so many people look at the Bible as just some list of rules that God gave us to make our lives miserable? Jesus came to bring freedom, not bondage! If you personally don't want to celebrate Christmas, don't do it. That's totally fine. And if you do want to celebrate Christmas, that's fine too. Don't feel bad or let others condemn you for your choice. My Bible says there is "no condemnation for those who are in Christ Jesus" (Rom. 8:1). If Jesus didn't come to condemn people, what makes us think it's our job?

God is way more concerned with your heart and the motives behind why you're doing what you do. Can you celebrate Christmas with your kids and family while still giving God the glory and honor? Absolutely you can. And you shouldn't feel bad at all when anyone else says otherwise.

It was a pagan holiday back in the day? OK, fine. That's not what it is in my house today! God sees my heart and my motives. And when we celebrate—telling our kids about the greatest gift ever given and that it had nothing to do with Santa and elves but everything to do with God sending His Son as a gift to the world so we all can be saved—God gets the glory! Not Santa. Not a pagan holiday.

Understand that the devil is the author and creator of nothing. Only God is the Creator. If the devil is using something for evil, that means God was using it for good first. I don't know about you, but I'll take anything the devil wants to use against me, turn it on him, and use it for the glory of God any day!

"Yeah, Kelly, but telling your kids Santa is bringing them gifts is straight-up lying. You can't show me anywhere in the Bible where that's OK!" You know what? You're absolutely right. Telling your kids Santa is bringing them gifts is lying. And there is no way to justify lying with the Bible. *So don't lie to your kids.* You can still have all the fun and joy of Christmas without lying. You do know there are other options, right? Why not tell them about St. Nicholas, who loved Jesus and loved bringing joy and helping others. You can still play the game of Santa without lying. Why do we as Christians make everything so difficult?

"OK, I see where you're coming from about Christmas, but Halloween is the devil's holiday. We shouldn't celebrate that, right?"

Now, I'm sure you may be sitting there saying, "Please say no. Please say no," or maybe you are saying, "Yep, it is! It's Satan's holiday. It's definitely a sin to celebrate Halloween." But again, I ask, What does the Bible say?

In the "Book of Judging Others 10:31," it plainly says, "You shall not trick-or-treat or wear costumes and have fun on Halloween." I'm kidding. But seriously, is it really Satan's holiday? "Um, yeah, Satan gets Halloween, and Jesus gets Christmas. That's how it works." You may think this sounds ridiculous, but let me tell you there are many people who believe exactly that.

You see, Psalm 118:24 says, "This is the day that the LORD has made; let us rejoice and be glad in it" (ESV).

So which day of the week is *this* referring to? *This* means *every single day* belongs to God. Satan doesn't get even one! Halloween is *not* Satan's holiday—unless you want to give it to him.

Satan doesn't have a day, nor does he want a day. What he wants is you. He wants to keep you so caught up in things that don't even matter—like whether Kanye West, Donald Trump, and Justin Bieber are really Christians. Once he has your mind focused on things like that, you have just become an ineffective Christian.

The only real weapon Satan has to use against you is to lie to you. And he can only hope for you to believe it. He wants nothing more than for you to picture him as some little red, evil guy with a pitchfork, just ready to stab you, when in reality Isaiah 14:15–17 says when we finally look down and see him in the pits of hell, we're going to say, in essence, "What? That's the guy? That's the dude that had us in such fear?" The truth is that he has nothing. He wants everything that you have. And he'll do whatever he can to get it, including keeping you so focused on the wrong things that you miss everything good God has for you.

"Yeah, but Halloween is just so evil! Kids dress up as scary demons and devils."

No doubt! So don't dress your kids up like that. The celebration of Halloween is not necessarily some big, evil day about worshipping the devil. It can simply be about your kids just having a fun time with family and friends and getting some candy. You get to choose if each day belongs to the Lord or to the devil. If you are looking for something to be good and search for the gold in it, you'll find it. If you are looking for something to be evil, well, you'll find that too. The real question is, What are you looking for?

Can Christians dress up, go trick-or-treating, and get candy while still giving honor to the Lord? Absolutely they can! Proverbs 13:22 says, "The wealth of the wicked is reserved for the righteous" (isv). Why can't the candy of the wicked as well be stored up for the righteous! (That was a joke—kind of.) Jesus even said the two most important commandments are to love your God and love your neighbor. How're you gonna love your neighbor if they come trick-or-treating, and you don't even open the door?

You see, I love my children. And when they dress up and go out with me to get candy from our neighbors, and they have a fun evening, we give glory to God. God wants you to have a good time. He wants you to have fun. He probably even wants you to have some candy! Not everything in the world has to always be evil and out to get you.

Remember, *this* is the day the Lord has made, and I *will* be glad and rejoice in it, even on Halloween! So in conclusion, is it a sin to celebrate Halloween? I guess it's all about why you're doing it. Just remember, whatever you choose to do, Satan doesn't have a day. He has nothing. He wants what you have. So I say let's give him nothing. What the world means for evil, we will take and use for good—all while giving glory to our Father!

Ultimately, it all comes down to what *you* believe

about Jesus. Everyone is living up to, or down to, the revelation of the freedom they have in Christ. We serve a good God who loves us and wants us to enjoy our lives here on earth, not just when we get to heaven. He's concerned with your heart and your motives. If you can celebrate Halloween and Christmas and all that comes with those holidays while still giving Him the glory and honor, go for it! Don't feel bad or ashamed just because someone else doesn't understand the freedom they have in Christ.

At the end of the day, the devil just wants to divide the body of Christ with stupid arguments about things that don't matter, because he knows if he can divide us, he can rob us of the power we have when we are united. Don't let the devil or anyone else rob you of your joy during the next holiday season. Have fun with your kids and family. Jesus is the reason for every season!

CHAPTER 13

Why Do I Feel So Wrong When I'm Doing Right?

HAVE YOU GIVEN your life to Jesus and committed to living as a Christian but still feel as though the devil beats you down daily? Despite your best efforts to follow Christ, you may find yourself overwhelmed, wondering what went wrong. Why does it feel as though the blessings you once enjoyed are now overshadowed by constant struggles? The answer may lie in where you are spiritually positioned. You could be standing outside God's protection without even realizing it.

Let's start out by exploring what I like to call God's umbrella of protection.

This concept is rooted in Psalm 91:9–11, which tells us, "If you make the LORD your refuge, if you make the Most High your shelter, no evil will conquer you; no plague will come near your home. For he will order his angels to protect you wherever you go" (NLT). Honestly, all of Psalm 91 provides a beautiful picture of God's protection and promise of safety and shelter for those who seek refuge in Him.

When you come under the Lord's protection, you find shelter in Him, and He promises to safeguard you from every harm. That is what it means to be under the *umbrella* of His protection. When you give your life to Jesus, you take your place under this incredible covering. His hand is on your life, and you begin to experience not only His protection but His blessings as well! Life feels good, you sense His presence, and everything seems to align as it should.

Until it doesn't.

You may have even experienced this yourself. You're serving God, attending church regularly, tithing, serving others, and doing everything you believe to be right. But suddenly, difficulties arise. Problems that were once occasional now seem to surface daily. You no longer feel as blessed, even though you know in your heart that you are. God feels distant, even though you know He hasn't moved. In these moments, we often ask ourselves, "What happened?"

The answer is simple.

We've stepped out from under God's umbrella of protection. And honestly, we don't even realize when it happens. We think we're doing everything right, but something shifts. So what causes us to leave that place of safety?

The Bible teaches that sin separates us from God. When we choose sin, whether consciously or not, we are choosing to step out from under His covering. God doesn't remove His protection; rather, we walk away from it by our own actions.

Once we step outside God's protection, the enemy has full access to attack us. The devil can't take away your salvation or send you to hell, but he can sure make your life here on earth feel like hell. And yet in our frustrations we often blame God. "Why is this happening to me?" we cry out. "Why is serving You so hard?" The reality is that serving God isn't hard. We *make* it hard. But to truly serve Him, all we have to do is *trust* Him. What could be easier than that? When we are fully convinced that His Word is true, and when we trust completely that His plan for us is better than ours, we *will* serve Him—not out of obligation but rather out of joy! However, stepping outside His protection is what makes life much harder than it needs to be.

In 1 Samuel 15:23 the Bible equates rebellion with witchcraft: "Rebellion is as the sin of witchcraft, and stubbornness is as iniquity and idolatry" (NKJV). At first glance this may seem shocking. "How can rebellion be compared to something as serious as witchcraft?" That is a great question.

And I have an answer!

Rebellion, in our culture, is often romanticized as a harmless act of independence or even a sign of strength. Many people take pride in being rebellious, thinking it's a way to assert control over their lives. I used to believe the same thing. Even after I gave my life to Jesus, I considered it cool to challenge authority and live by my own rules. "I do what I want," I thought, and I took pride in not conforming. But rebellion isn't just about living life on your own terms, is it? When we knowingly go against God's Word, we are really saying, "I know what God's Word says, but my way is better." And we are acting in rebellion. Rebellion is essentially saying, "God, I know better than You. I know You said this is wrong, but I'm going to do it anyway."

Ouch.

This mindset is extremely dangerous because you can serve only one master, either God or the devil. When you knowingly oppose God's Word and choose your way over His, you are, in effect, serving the enemy. Call it pride. Call it tradition. Call it insecurity—whatever label you place on it, it's rebellion. For example, you may want to justify your actions by saying, "This is how my family has always done it," or, "I don't want to come across as too religious." But if you've given your life to Jesus yet continue to knowingly walk in sin, you have stepped out from under God's protective umbrella.

The Bible tells us that weapons will be formed against us, but they will not prosper (Isa. 54:17). That promise holds true as long as we remain under God's protection. However, when we step out of alignment with His will, we lose that protective covering, leaving ourselves vulnerable to attacks of the enemy.

Now, you may be thinking, "I'm not living in sin. I've changed. I'm not the person I used to be." And that may be true. You may have turned away from the big, obvious sins like drinking, swearing, lying, and stealing. But here is where many miss the mark. We tend to categorize sins, seeing some as big and others as insignificant. We dismiss certain behaviors as struggles rather than recognizing them for what they really are—sin.

The enemy thrives on this deception. God doesn't see big sins and little sins. He simply sees sin. Whether it's bitterness, unforgiveness, pride, gossip, or offense, if you allow these things into your life, you are still stepping out from under God's umbrella of protection. And when you allow sin to linger in your heart, you give the enemy a foothold.

This may be a fresh revelation for you. You may be realizing that the struggles you've been facing aren't just random attacks from the enemy but the result of unrecognized sin in your life. If you're recognizing that now, the good news is that you're in the perfect place to make a change.

Jesus died to make it easy for us to remain under God's protection. He has already paid the price for your sins, and because of that you can draw as close to God as you want. James 4:8 tells us, "Draw near to God and He will draw near to you" (NKJV). The first step is always on us. But don't be afraid that every mistake will instantly remove you from God's protection. We all sin and make mistakes, and there is grace for that. However, there is a difference between making a mistake and choosing to live in sin.

The key to staying under God's protection is repentance. Repentance is not simply saying, "I'm sorry." It's a complete change of mind that leads you to a change in your direction. Repentance means turning away from sin and realigning yourself with God's Word. When you truly repent, you step back under the umbrella of God's protection.

Repentance is more than an emotional moment at the altar. It's not about shedding tears or feeling remorseful. True repentance is reflected in a changed life. It's when you not only acknowledge your sin but also commit to living differently. If you think you can fool God by simply saying *sorry* every time you sin without truly changing, you're only deceiving yourself. God knows the condition of your heart.

While it's true that Jesus' sacrifice guarantees our salvation, remaining in sin allows the enemy to wreak havoc on our lives. You may be heaven bound, but your life here on earth could feel like a constant battle. The only reason anyone would remain outside God's protection is that they believe the world offers something better than what Jesus has to give. Yet God's Word is clear—nothing in this world can compare to the love, peace, and protection we find in Him.

So let me encourage you today!

If you recognize that you've stepped outside God's umbrella of protection, know that returning is as simple as a single step. God loves you so deeply, He has a plan for your life, and He wants to protect you. I say we let Him! Nothing in this world can offer you what Jesus can. Don't give the enemy access to your life by allowing small struggles (which are really sins) to persist. Identify them, remove them, and step back under God's umbrella of protection.

Living under God's umbrella doesn't mean your life will be free from challenges, but it does mean that no weapon formed against you will prosper. There is no safer or more fulfilling place to stand than under His protective covering. Take that step back today, and experience the peace and security that come from being in the center of His will.

CHAPTER 14

Do We Have to Pray Out Loud?

WHEN WE PRAY, do we need to speak the words out loud, or can we just say our prayers in our heads? This question resonates deeply with many people who have wondered about the mechanics of communication with God. I'll never forget a pivotal moment in my life when I was driving and God spoke to me directly. He said, "Kelly, if every word you spoke came true, would it change the way you speak?"

I paused, reflecting on this powerful question, and then answered, "Yes, God, of course it would. If every word I spoke came true, I would absolutely change how I speak."

And God responded, "Then change the way you speak."

I know we've already touched on this earlier in the book, but this concept is so monumental, so life altering, that it bears repeating. Sometimes hearing something multiple times allows it to truly sink in, and I believe this principle has the power to transform your life.

Let's take a moment to revisit a foundational truth

from the Bible. Genesis 1:27 tells us we are made in the image of God. Think about that for a moment. Whose image are we created in? We are made in the image of God. Yes, I'm repeating that because it's such an extraordinary truth. You were created in the likeness of the Almighty!

But why is this such a big deal?

It's a big deal because of how God creates. He speaks. When God wanted to create the heavens and the earth, He spoke them into existence. This is the divine method of creation: words. And because we are made in His image, the same principle applies to us. Our words have the power to create. When we speak, we are shaping the world around us. Just as when God speaks, the universe must come into alignment with His words, so too when we speak, our words have the potential to affect our reality.

Do you realize how life-changing this is? If you find yourself unhappy today with the circumstances of your life, the hard truth is that you have likely spoken those circumstances into existence. That's difficult to hear, I know. But here's the good news: If your words got you into this situation, your words can get you out. By changing the way you speak, you can change the reality that surrounds you.

You may be thinking, "But I'm just speaking what I see. I'm not going to lie to myself and pretend things are good when they aren't. I'm just acknowledging the facts." That's the problem right there. The Bible defines *faith* in Hebrews 11:1—"Faith shows the reality of what we hope for; it is the evidence of things we cannot see" (NLT). This means that faith isn't about speaking what is visible or tangible; it's about speaking what isn't yet seen as though it already exists.

Can you pray silently in your head? Absolutely! God is most concerned with the condition of your heart, and He hears you no matter what. However, once you understand the immense power that lies in speaking out your words, you should feel compelled to pray out loud as much as you can. Spoken words carry an authority that silent thoughts do not.

I've heard some people say, "I don't want to pray out loud, because I don't want the enemy to hear my prayers and use them against me." At first glance this seems like a valid concern. But let's unpack that for a moment. Is that thought rooted in faith or fear? You see, when you say, "I don't want the devil to hear my prayers," what you're really saying is, "God, You're powerful, but not as powerful as the enemy." Ouch, right? No one would ever say those words aloud, but many think and act that way without realizing it.

I want the enemy to hear my prayers. I want him to know that I'm fully aware of what God can do in my life. I want him to know that I'm coming for him because I stand under the protection of a victorious God. The devil is already defeated! The only power he has is what we give him. So don't give him more power by being afraid to speak your prayers aloud.

Remember, the enemy can't stop what God is doing or plans to do in your life unless you let him. Don't allow fear to keep you silent. Instead, declare your prayers boldly and with authority, knowing that God's power far exceeds anything the enemy can throw your way.

Here's another secret to supercharging your prayers: When you pray, speak God's Word back to Him. Incorporating Scripture into your prayers is one of the most powerful things you can do. You may wonder, "Why would I need to remind God of His Word? Doesn't He already know it? After all, He wrote it." And while that may seem like a logical question, the answer is crucial. It's not about reminding God; it's about activating the power of His Word in your life.

Our words by themselves don't have any intrinsic power. But God's Word? That's a different story! Every word from God is charged with power. When you align your prayers with Scripture, you are tapping into the very power of God Himself.

Think of it like this: When you pray God's Word, you are agreeing with what God has already declared to be true, and that agreement releases supernatural power into your situation.

If you've followed me online or watched any of my videos, you've probably heard me say this a thousand times, but I'll keep saying it because it's that important. Every single promise in God's Word is "yes" and "amen" for your life (2 Cor. 1:20). But here's the catch: The promises are not automatic. You have to go after them. How? By reading the Bible, discovering God's promises, and then reminding Him of them in prayer.

You may be wondering, "Where can I find these

promises? Is there a specific book or chapter in the Bible where they're all listed?" The truth is that there isn't one central location. The promises of God are woven throughout the entire Bible. Here's how it works: When you see God doing something for someone in the Bible and need Him to do the same for you, you pray that promise. Or when you read a scripture that instructs you to ask for faith, wisdom, peace, or provision, you can claim that promise by praying it over your life and *thanking* Him that He's already given it to you. This is how you pray with faith.

For instance, if you were in need of provision, you might say something like, "God, I see in 2 Kings that You provided for the widow who had only a little bit of oil. You multiplied it and met all her needs, giving her even more than enough. Lord, I know You are the same yesterday, today, and forever. What You did for her, I trust You will do for me. Thank You, God, that You are my provider and that You have already made a way for me!"

Do you see how easy this is?

In this way, you're praying God's Word right back to Him. This is how you lay hold of His promises.

The most important takeaway is this: Pray as much as you can! God delights in communicating with you, whether it's silent or spoken. But when possible, pray out loud. Remember, there is immense power in your spoken words because you are created in the image of a God who speaks things into existence. Don't be afraid of the enemy hearing your prayers. Instead, let him hear! Let him know you aren't afraid of him. Keep reminding him that he's already been defeated by the King of kings. Turn the very weapons he tries to use against you into testimonies of God's faithfulness.

So if every word you spoke came true, would it change the way you speak? If the answer is yes, then it's time to change the way you speak.

CHAPTER 15

Does the Principle of Tithing Still Apply to Christians Today?

DO CHRISTIANS REALLY have to give 10 percent of their income back to the church? Or is this just a clever trick of the churches to make money? I've taught on this topic, so if this question has been on your mind, let's answer three questions:

1. Do the tithing scriptures in the Bible even apply to us today?

2. When the Bible mentions tithing, is it actually talking about money?

3. Does the tithe *have* to go to the church?

Together, let's answer these three questions using the Word of God and see if we can bring some clarity on this topic.

The main tithing scriptures that pastors, teachers, and almost everyone use are found in Malachi 3:8–10 (NKJV).

"Will a man rob God? Yet you have robbed Me! But
you say, 'In what way have we robbed You?' In tithes
and offerings. You are cursed with a curse, for you
have robbed Me, even this whole nation. Bring all
the tithes into the storehouse, that there may be
food in My house, and try Me now in this," says the
LORD of hosts, "if I will not open for you the win-
dows of heaven and pour out for you such blessing
that there will not be room enough to receive it."

I don't know about you, but that sounds amazing to me!

"But does it apply to us?" you say. "That's the Old
Testament. Don't we follow the New Covenant and the
New Testament? I'm pretty sure this isn't for us today."

While teaching on tithing, I have heard this reply
more times than I can count. And it always blows my
mind. If we're basing this off the Old Testament argument, then why does Malachi 3:6 (NKJV) begin with the
statement "For I am the LORD, I do not change"? In fact,
over one hundred times, the Bible says that God doesn't
change. Hmm. For us to say tithing doesn't apply to us
today is very interesting. It seems to me that God saw
this argument coming before we did!

Seriously, though, let's think about this for a minute.

Do we just throw out the Ten Commandments now
too? Because that's Old Testament as well. "Jesus died for
my sins! They've all been paid for! Woo-hoo! Murdering
is just fine then."

Come on, now. That's ridiculous.

I'll be honest with you, though. I wish Malachi 3 *was*
in the New Testament. That would save me so much time

and eliminate so many arguments. Because I've heard this a lot too: "You can't use only the New Testament to prove that Jesus wants us to tithe! It's impossible, Kelly."

Oh, really?

Malachi is the last Book in the Old Testament. Matthew is the first Book in the New Testament. I've often said, "God, if You could have just moved this tithing chapter one book over from Malachi, it would have fixed everything."

But check this out.

While going through Bible college, one of my professors asked me to use only the New Testament to write a paper that proves that we are still called to tithe. My heart sank. At the time I also thought it couldn't be done. I remember thinking, "My professor wouldn't have asked me to do this if it couldn't be done." I started at Matthew 1:1 and decided I would read through the entire New Testament, on a mission to find some verse or passage I could use to teach that Jesus didn't do away with the tithe. And, my friend, let me tell you—it didn't take long before I struck pure gold.

Matthew 23:23 changed everything!

Now I refer to this verse as the tithing slam dunk because this is the Michael Jordan of tithing scriptures. In this verse, Jesus is speaking. Not Paul. Not a disciple. Jesus Himself. He's talking to the Pharisees, the religious rulers who tried to live by the Old Testament Law (or just the Law to them at the time) because they thought that was what would give them access to salvation. And here's what Jesus said to them in verse 23:

What sorrow awaits you teachers of religious law and you Pharisees. Hypocrites! For you are careful to tithe even the tiniest income from your herb gardens, but you ignore the more important aspects of the law—justice, mercy, and faith. You should tithe, yes, but do not neglect the more important things.

—MATTHEW 23:23, NLT

What? In the New Testament? Out of Jesus' own mouth? Well, there you go. Jesus Himself says that yes, "you should tithe." Did He say tithing is the most important thing? No, but you still should be doing it.

I don't care what anybody else has ever told you. If there's one person whose opinion should matter, it's Jesus. And what's His opinion on this subject? You should be tithing!

In Matthew 5:17 Jesus says, "I have not come to abolish [the laws] but to fulfill them."

I love that Malachi 3, in the New Living Translation, has the heading "A Call to Repentance," because repentance means you change your mind *and* your direction.

Do we need to tithe? Absolutely we do. But why? Let's keep going.

Does *tithe* refer to our money, or can it include gifts and time as well?

I've heard many people say, "I give my time as my tithe. I gave a car. I give food to the hungry. I donate clothes to shelters. I don't give my money, because God doesn't need it, but people do." But do those things actually count as tithing?

Let's go back to Malachi 3 again.

Malachi 3:8 (NKJV) says, "In what way have we robbed you?" God replies, "In tithes *and* offerings" (emphasis added). Take note, these are two different and separate things. The tithe has always meant one-tenth. Income back then looked a lot different than it does today. I mean, I don't think you're getting paid in sheep and wheat or goats and oils. But the principle remains the same. One-tenth of your income—that's a tithe. Does the tithe mean money? Yes, it does. But remember, the scripture says, in essence, "You have robbed Me in tithes *and* offerings." While a tithe is 10 percent of your income, your offering can be anything you want!

Think of it like this: Your tithe, the 10 percent, is a key that unlocks the door to give God access to your finances. If you're praying for a financial miracle or blessing but aren't tithing, you're essentially asking God to do a work in your life in an area He has no access to. The offering, however, is everything that God blesses abundantly on top of what you're already giving. Does that make sense?

The abundant blessings promised in Malachi 3 aren't tied to the tithe alone. The tithe unlocks the door for God to have access to bless your finances, but the *abundant* blessings come from what you give above and beyond your tithe.

This was brilliantly set up by our Father so that both those who have plenty and those who have nothing have access to the same abundant blessings. If you make a million dollars, your tithe is 10 percent. If you make one hundred dollars, your tithe is 10 percent. The key to unlocking the door to bless you is 10 percent. Then the measure of how or how much you get blessed is based not on money but rather on your heart. Your offering will always be attached to your heart. Your tithe will be based solely on your income. However, offerings can be your money, your time, or your possessions, or something else. The point is, however you sow whatever you sow is the same way you will reap. This means the attitude or heart posture you have when giving above and beyond your tithe, no matter what it is you are giving, is the same attitude God will use when giving to your life.

"OK, but why didn't Jesus just explain this like you are? That would have made things so much easier."

The best answer I have for you is that Jesus didn't need to spend all His time teaching on the tithe, because we were already supposed to have that down! To the people of His day this was common knowledge, and it should be for us too. Remember, Jesus told the Pharisees, "Yes, you should be tithing." Jesus didn't go around constantly saying not to murder people either. We just know we don't do that. We should also just know we ought to be tithing.

"OK, I'm supposed to tithe. And the tithe *is* money. But now the question is, Does my tithe actually have to go to the church?"

Again, the Scripture says, "Bring the whole tithe into the storehouse, that there may be food in my house" (Mal. 3:10). Your tithes should go to the church you belong to. The storehouse in this verse represents our modern church today. And the scripture makes it crystal clear that this is where the tithe goes. I've had many people ask me, "Can I tithe to different ministries if I'm a member at [insert name here] Church?" I like to respond by saying, "We go to church to feed on the Word of God. So tithe where you get fed." Like, I dare you to go to a restaurant this Sunday after church, order your meal, finish the food, and then tell the waitress you're going to pay the restaurant across town because you actually like that one better.

That's ridiculous, right? That's how this works.

Where you're getting fed is where your tithe should go. Now, your offering? That's another story altogether. Offerings can go anywhere you want. You want to sow into Kelly K Ministries? You can! (I'm only kidding, but you get the point.) Offerings are what you give out of your heart above and beyond your 10 percent. Ten percent goes to the church. The rest goes wherever you want.

"Kelly, I'm just not sure about giving my money to a church. How can I trust that they are using the money correctly? So many pastors and churches are corrupt these days. I want to make sure my money is really going to help build the kingdom."

This is a very legitimate thought and concern.

However, let me share an amazing secret with you. When you start giving to honor the Lord, you don't give horizontally—you give vertically. This means when you give your tithe or offering, it feels as if you're giving it to that church, pastor, or ministry. But in reality, you're giving it to God. God is looking at your heart and motives for giving. What that church does with the money, they will have to answer for. You will have to answer for how well you obeyed, and they will have to answer for how well they stewarded what you gave.

At this point, you may be getting hung up, thinking, "But didn't you say there's a curse coming to me if I choose not to give my tithe and offering?" That is true. The Bible does say you are cursed if you don't tithe (Mal. 3:9).

"What kind of mean God would curse me if I don't give Him my money?"

Please understand this. When the Bible says in this verse that you've robbed God, it's not talking about your money. What it means is that you've robbed the Lord of an opportunity to bless you! God is saying, "If you give Me access to your finances, I'm going to bless you. And not only will I bless you; I will bless you so much you won't even be able to hold it all." This world is already cursed. When you give your life to Jesus, however, you step under His umbrella of protection and out from under the curse. (We discussed this in chapter 13 of this book.) And when you don't tithe, you step out from under God's umbrella of protection. He didn't curse you. You walked into the curse. God is saying here, "Don't rob Me of a chance to bless your life financially and in every other possible way!"

Essentially, your tithing just shows God that He alone is your God, not money. When you tithe, you are letting God know, "I give You access to all my life, including this area that's extremely hard to do. What the world says I need to chase after, I give to You. You are all I need!"

I have lived a life where I didn't tithe, and I've lived a life where I tithe consistently. There is a huge difference. That's not to mention, this is the only place in the Bible where God says, "Test Me!" Are you kidding me? God is essentially triple-dog daring you to tithe! He is so confident in His promise and desire to bless you that He is daring you to try and see for yourself!

So if you're on the fence about the tithe, and if you haven't tried it yet, let me challenge you today. Take the advice of Jesus in Matthew 23:23. Yes! You *should* be tithing. God gave you a promise and then raised the stakes with a dare. I say try it out, and see what happens!

CHAPTER 16

Do All Dogs Go to Heaven?

D O ALL DOGS really go to heaven? Or any pets, for that matter? It's a question that's been asked by many, especially those of us who have loved and lost a furry friend. The idea of animals, especially pets, having a place in eternity is both comforting and intriguing.

Hollywood certainly hasn't shied away from the idea. Remember the movie *All Dogs Go to Heaven* that we all loved as kids? Burt Reynolds voiced the charming and mischievous Charlie, a dog who, after some twists and turns, finds himself in heaven. One of the most emotional scenes in the movie is when the little girl asks, "Charlie, will I ever see you again?" He replies, "Sure you will, kid. You know goodbyes aren't forever." It's a line that has definitely stuck with me over the years.

It's hard not to hope that our pets will be waiting for us in eternity, but we have to ask ourselves, "Is that what really happens?"

We can enjoy the comforting narrative of a children's

movie, but what does the Bible say about this matter? To understand the role of animals in eternity, we need to dive into Scripture and see what God says about the creation, purpose, and ultimate destiny of both humans and animals.

Let's begin with the creation account in Genesis 1. This chapter is a fundamental text that reveals God's creative power and His intentions for all life on earth. On the fifth day God created the animals that inhabited the water. Then on the sixth day He created land-dwelling animals. He commanded the earth to produce "all the creatures that move along the ground," and after this the scripture says, "And God saw that it was good" (v. 25; see also vv. 20–24). Clearly, animals are part of God's good creation. However, something unique happens when God creates humans. In verse 27 we read, "God created human beings in his own image. In the image of God he created them; male and female he created them" (NLT).

This is an important distinction.

Humans are set apart from the rest of creation because they are made in God's image. No other creature, not even the animals God declared to be good, are said to share this divine image. This sets humans apart in a profound way, and it hints at the idea that humans have a special destiny that animals do not share.

In addition to this, the Bible teaches that humans are made of three parts: flesh, soul, and spirit (1 Thess. 5:23). Just as God is a three-part Being (Father, Son, and Holy Spirit), humans reflect this nature in their own three-part design.

Our flesh is the physical part of us—the part that lives, breathes, and interacts with the world around us. However, it's also the part that is tainted by sin and that remains on the earth when we die. Your soul is composed of your mind, will, and emotions. This is the part of us that we must "take captive" every day, as the Bible teaches (2 Cor. 10:5), so we can control our thoughts and actions. Then there is your spirit, the part of you that connects directly with God. When someone accepts Jesus into their heart, it is their spirit that is made perfect, and it is this part that goes to heaven. Our spirits, along with our souls, will ascend to heaven when we die, but our flesh will remain here on earth.

"Yeah, Kelly, but what about animals?"

Animals, like humans, do have flesh. They also have minds, wills, and emotions. Anyone who has had a pet knows that animals can think, decide, and feel, even if their understanding is far simpler than ours. However, animals are not made in the image of God, and more importantly, they don't have spirits.

"Oh no! Are you telling me that Fluffy isn't in heaven?"

Hold on just a second before jumping to conclusions. Let's not bark at this idea without examining it a little more. (See what I did there?)

While it's true that animals lack spirits, the Bible does not leave us completely without hope when it comes to our pets. Let's dive into some other scriptures that may shed more light on this issue.

First, let's look at Psalm 36:6, which says, "You care for people and animals alike, O LORD" (NLT). This verse shows us that God has a deep love for His creation, including the animals. God is a loving caretaker for both humans and animals, and this should bring you some comfort. God cares for all creatures, and this love is part of the goodness of His creation.

Also, Psalm 148 contains even more intriguing verses. It says, "Praise the LORD...wild animals and all cattle, small creatures and flying birds" (vv. 7, 10). These verses, along with others like them, suggest that animals not only are capable of praising God but actually *are* praising Him in their own way! Several scriptures indicate that animals, in their simple and instinctual lives, bring glory to God just by being what He created them to be. This opens the door to the possibility that animals may have a more significant spiritual role than we thought.

We also need to address a key distinction in our question. The question we're asking is not whether there will be animals in heaven but whether our specific *pets* will be there. From the Bible it seems far more likely that there will be animals in heaven than not. Several passages in Scripture appear to describe animals being present in eternity.

For instance, in Isaiah 11:6–9 and Isaiah 65:25 we read about a future peaceful kingdom where animals will live together in harmony. These passages describe a time when "the wolf will live with the lamb, [and] the leopard will lie down with the goat" (Isa. 11:6). This imagery of peace and unity among animals seems to refer to an eternal state. The presence of animals in this future suggests that God *does* choose to include animals in the new heaven and new earth.

However, there is some pushback with other parts of Scripture. Isaiah 35:9 suggests that in eternity, "no lion will be there, nor any ravenous beast." This verse could be interpreted in different ways, but it presents a contrast to the idea of all animals living in eternity. Additionally, in Revelation 19:11–16 we see Jesus riding on a white horse, an image that suggests at least *some* animals are present in the heavenly realm.

From these passages it seems reasonable to conclude that animals will exist in heaven.

"Stop beating around the bush, man! Just tell us already. What about our pets? Will Fluffy, Scruffy, or Garfield be there?"

I know you are looking for a specific answer here, but this is where things get a bit more uncertain. Let's explore some possibilities.

It's difficult to imagine eternity without the faithful companions who have been such important parts of our lives. While the Bible does not explicitly say that our pets will be in heaven, I believe we should consider the character of God when reflecting on this issue.

Isn't God good? Doesn't He love you more than anything? If your pet played a vital role in your life or just brought you pure joy, why wouldn't a loving God allow you to experience that same joy in eternity? God knows what brings us happiness, and He delights in giving us good gifts. It's not unreasonable at all to believe that if having your dog or cat with you in heaven would bring you joy, God could make that happen.

We must also remember that heaven will be a place of perfect peace, joy, and contentment. Everything we need to be completely happy will be provided. If having your beloved pet with you is part of that joy, then I have no doubt God could make that a reality. God delights in giving His children good things, and the Bible assures us that heaven is a place where every tear will be wiped away (Rev. 21:4). If being reunited with your pets would bring you joy and comfort, then I believe it is entirely possible.

We live in a fallen world, and death is a painful part of that reality. The loss of a pet is heartbreaking, but take comfort in knowing that death is not the end. For those who trust in Jesus, death has been defeated, and we will one day live in a world free of sorrow, pain, and death. In that new world, who knows what surprises God may have in store for us.

I know I can't wait to find out!

So the next time you have to say goodbye to a pet, take comfort in the possibility that "goodbyes aren't forever." While we may not know all the details about what eternity holds, we can trust in the goodness of God. He loves you, He cares about your happiness, and He knows how much you love your pet. Whether or not our pets will be waiting for us in heaven, we can be confident of one thing: In heaven all will be made right, and we will experience a joy that goes beyond anything we can even imagine.

CHAPTER 17

Is Baptism Required to Get into Heaven?

THE QUESTION OF whether baptism is required to get into heaven is one that has stirred debate among Christians for centuries. It's a question that carries deep spiritual implications and often causes an emotional response. The arguments usually fall into two distinct camps: One side believes that baptism is essential for salvation, while the other maintains that belief in Jesus alone is sufficient. Both perspectives have biblical support, and it is crucial to examine the Bible carefully to form an understanding of what God actually requires of us for salvation.

Let me begin by stating that what follows is my interpretation based on Scripture. However, this topic, like many in Christianity, is a matter of significant division among believers. Therefore, I encourage you to not only consider what I share here but to read and study the Bible yourself to come to your own conclusion. It's important to approach topics like this with an open heart and a willingness to seek God's truth rather than just rely on someone else's interpretation. In fact, this principle should apply to every teaching and doctrine you come across on your journey of faith.

Before we just give a yes or no to whether baptism is necessary for salvation, it's essential to understand what baptism is and what it symbolizes. For those new to Christianity, baptism typically involves being submerged in water by a pastor or preacher. The individual being baptized is asked if they believe in Jesus Christ and that He came to earth and died for their sins. Upon affirmation the pastor will then say something like, "I now baptize you in the name of the Father, the Son, and the Holy Spirit." Then the pastor will dunk the person briefly under the water before bringing them back up.

This act may seem strange at first, especially if you're unfamiliar with Christian traditions. So why do Christians do this? What is the significance of baptism?

Baptism is extremely symbolic. The Bible teaches that we must die to ourselves daily and be "crucified with Christ" (Gal. 2:20; see also Luke 9:23). Of course, this doesn't mean a literal death, but rather a spiritual one. We are called to die to our old, sinful ways and be reborn into a new life in Christ. Going under the water during baptism represents this death to the old self, and emerging from the water represents the new life in Christ. It is an outward sign of an inward transformation.

However, many people mistakenly think of baptism as our testimony *to* God, showing Him what we've done for Him. But this couldn't be further from the truth. In fact, baptism is God's testimony to us! It is a physical sign of the salvation He has made possible through the work of Jesus Christ and the ongoing work of the Holy Spirit. It is a testimony to the salvation God has already accomplished for us.

Baptism is, however, a command from God—much like the command to take Communion. These are both practices that believers are called to follow, in remembrance of what Jesus has done for us and to publicly show our faith in God. The Bible clearly teaches that we are saved by grace, through faith, not by works. Acts 16:31 says, "Believe in the Lord Jesus, and you will be saved." Ephesians 2:8–9 adds, "For it is by grace you have been saved, through faith—and this is not from yourselves, it is the gift of God—not by works, so that no one can boast."

The Bible makes it clear that salvation comes through faith in Jesus Christ. You must believe that Jesus is the Son of God and that He came to earth, died for your sins, and rose again. Once you believe this, you are called to repent of your sins, which means not just feeling sorry for them but turning away from them and living in a way that pleases God. Repentance is about aligning your desires with God's, loving what He loves, and hating what He hates. God loves people and hates sin. True repentance should bring about a change in your thoughts and actions, leading you to live in a way that honors God.

So when answering the question "Do I have to be

baptized to get into heaven?" one of the best biblical examples we can look to is the thief on the cross. As Jesus was being crucified, one of the criminals hanging beside Him said, "Jesus, remember me when you come into your kingdom" (Luke 23:42). This man acknowledged Jesus as his Savior and asked for His mercy, even though he was moments away from death. Jesus responded, "Truly I tell you, today you will be with me in paradise" (v. 43).

Let's break this down.

The thief had no opportunity to be baptized. He didn't have the time to attend any church services, give any offerings, take a single communion, or even try to live a life of obedience to God's Word. Yet Jesus assured him that he would be in heaven. This shows us that while baptism is important, it is not a requirement for salvation. The thief's faith and repentance were enough for Jesus to promise him eternal life.

Baptism, though not required for salvation, is a vital and meaningful act of obedience for every believer. It is a symbol of the believer's new identity in Christ and a public declaration of their faith. The Bible encourages all believers to be baptized as a way of following Jesus' example and demonstrating their commitment to Him. Jesus Himself was baptized, not because He needed to be saved but because He wanted to set an example for us to follow.

If someone accepts Jesus as their Savior but doesn't have the opportunity to be baptized, they are not at risk of losing their salvation. God's grace is not dependent on our abilities to perform specific rituals. However, if someone *chooses* not to be baptized out of indifference, rebellion, or disbelief, that attitude may reflect a deeper issue with their heart and their willingness to submit to God's authority.

Baptism should be the norm for every believer. It is a significant and transformative act that solidifies the believer's relationship with Christ and that publicly affirms their faith. If a believer understands what baptism represents and chooses to disregard it, that decision may indicate a refusal to fully commit to God's plan for their life.

Since baptism is such a powerful and meaningful experience, the real question becomes, Why wouldn't you want to be baptized? Baptism is a public testimony that you are dying to your old self and committing your life to Christ. It shows the entire world that you are serious about following Jesus and living according to His teachings. Baptism is a beautiful way to symbolize the transformation that has taken place in your life. Just writing about it makes me want to get baptized again!

Jesus says, "Whoever acknowledges me before others, I will also acknowledge before my Father in heaven. But whoever disowns me before others, I will disown before my Father in heaven" (Matt. 10:32–33). Baptism is one way we acknowledge Jesus before others. It's an outward demonstration of the inward reality that we have been crucified with Christ and raised to new life in Him.

At this point you may be wondering if you need to be baptized again. Perhaps you were baptized as a child but didn't fully understand the significance at the time. Or maybe you were baptized as an adult, not because it meant anything to you but because you were told to. The answer to this question depends on your current understanding of baptism. If you were baptized as an infant or a young child but now, as an adult, have come to a deeper understanding of what it means, then go for it! God is looking at your heart, remember?

I was baptized when I was eighteen years old, but I didn't fully grasp the significance of the act at that time. I did it because I was told it was the right thing to do. Years later, after serving as a pastor for over a decade, I chose to be baptized again. This time I did it with a full understanding of its importance and meaning. I wanted to publicly declare my commitment to Christ in front of my own congregation and acknowledge that baptism is a command from God that I take seriously. And you know what? It was amazing!

If you feel that your understanding of baptism has deepened since your first baptism, there is nothing wrong with being baptized again. It can be a powerful and affirming experience that reinforces your faith and dedication to Christ.

In conclusion, baptism is an extremely important decision for all believers. But it is not a requirement for salvation. Salvation comes through faith in Jesus Christ, repentance, and the grace of God. The story of the thief on the cross shows us that even without baptism, a heart that believes and repents can still receive the promise of eternal life. That being said, baptism is a command from God and an essential part of the Christian walk. It is a public declaration of faith and an act of obedience that every believer should participate in if given the opportunity.

CHAPTER 18

On Which Day Are We Supposed to Honor the Sabbath?

I F YOU'VE BEEN a Christian for any length of time, I'm sure you've found yourself caught in this debate. And if you haven't, give it time. You will! It seems not a single day goes by without someone asking me this. I've heard such a mixed bag of responses.

Is the Sabbath supposed to be on Saturday? "Yep! It's absolutely Saturday. That was the Jewish Sabbath, and that's what the Bible says. Any other day is wrong in the eyes of the Lord. How dare you go to church on Sunday!" That is a real response that was left in my comments. But let me ask, If this is true, then why do so many Christians—most, actually—go to church on Sunday?

"That's easy, Kelly. Because it doesn't matter which day you go. Jesus changed everything, and now we just go. The day isn't important at all." Let's be honest, both of those arguments sound valid. On one hand, the Bible does teach that the Jews observed the Sabbath on Saturday. On the other hand, Jesus did change every-thing. So what is the truth? Which day is correct? You already know, but I'm going to say it anyway—*I'm so glad you asked!*

To start, let's make sure we understand what the Sabbath is.

In Genesis, at the very beginning, we see God creating the world in six days, and on the seventh day He rests. Then later, in Exodus, we see God give Moses the Ten Commandments. One of those commandments tells us, "Remember the Sabbath day by keeping it holy" (Exod. 20:8). So what *is* the Sabbath? The Sabbath is a day of rest. Now, pay attention to what I said—a day of rest. Not the day to go to church! So right out of the gate, if someone is wondering which day they are supposed to go to church, because that's the Sabbath, they've missed it.

Sabbath means a day of rest, and the Bible tells us we are supposed to keep it holy. And what does *holy* mean? It means to be set apart for God, or to be set apart for use *by* God. So let's put those puzzle pieces together. We are commanded to have a day of rest and to keep that day set apart for God or for use by God. That's the Sabbath! But that didn't give us the answer of which day it's supposed to be.

Let's go back to the Bible.

Biblically, as we discussed already, the Sabbath was Saturday. Sunday is the first day of the week; Saturday is the last. God worked six days and took a rest on day seven. "Yep, I knew it! Thank you, Kelly, for finally setting these people straight. The true Sabbath is Saturday. That's when we go to church, not Sunday."

Now, hold your horses there a minute. Again, I say to you, it's not about which day you go to church. Let's look at what Jesus says in Mark 2. Here we find Jesus and His disciples walking through some grain fields on the Sabbath, and they start breaking off heads of grain to eat. The Pharisees are watching them, and when they see this happen, they lose their ever-loving minds. I can only imagine how this scene played out. They probably started pointing and shouting, "Oh, look! Look! They're breaking the Law! Jesus and His disciples are harvesting grain on the Sabbath! How dare they! We got 'em now, boys. You can't be harvesting on the Sabbath. Shame on You!" Honestly, that sounds like a lot of people I know today. But then Jesus replies, "The Sabbath was made to meet the needs of people, and not people to meet the requirements of the Sabbath" (v. 27, NLT).

You see, here is what we miss all the time. The Sabbath is a *gift* from God to us. Jesus says the Sabbath's purpose is "to meet the needs of people." This means you need a day off. You need a day of rest. And that day needs to be kept holy, set apart for God.

"Dude, quit dancing around the main point, and just tell us already. What day is the Sabbath supposed to be?"

Any. Day. You. Want.

The problem with the Pharisees in Jesus' day, and with a lot of believers today as well, sadly, is that they tried to turn the Bible (or the Law) into a god itself. They worshipped the Law instead of the One who gave it. And if you stop and think long enough, I guarantee you'll come up with a few people you know who seem to have done this as well. It's way more common than you may think, and I believe these people don't even realize that's what they've done. I know they have good intentions. It's just that, like the Pharisees, they are *deceived*. They look at the Bible as if it's a list of rules they have to follow. And if you don't follow every single rule to completion, shame on you!

But please understand this: Jesus didn't come to bring you more bondage; He came to set you free. The Bible is not just some book of rules you have to follow to get into heaven. It is the greatest love letter ever written—a love letter written to you from the Creator of the universe! Every single word in the Bible is there to bring you freedom, not bondage. It sets you free; it doesn't turn you into a slave. But the thing is, you have to let it. It was us, human beings, who messed this all up. We turned a gift from God into a religious law that we "have" to follow about which day of the week we go to church.

Facepalm.

It's embarrassing when you really think about it. The truth is, *we* are the church. We go to a building we call a church for the purpose of being trained and equipped so we can leave that building and go out and actually *be* the church! I don't want to offend you today, but I'm going to get really honest with you right now. You going to church is not you *serving* God. You can be a servant at church, but the act of you going does not serve God. You serve God on your way to church and then everywhere you go when you walk out the door! Your time inside that building? That's boot camp. That's school. That's training. Is this starting to click?

And to be very real and transparent with you, this commandment right here is one of my greatest struggles. I *love* to work. It doesn't hurt that I have the greatest job in the world. But it doesn't matter. Even though my work is preaching and teaching the gospel, I still have to remember God told me I need a day of rest and I need to keep it holy—set apart for Him. I just love making videos! I love writing books! I love traveling and speaking and preaching! I just don't ever want to stop.

Here is what I want you to see. The devil would love to get us caught up doing "good" things for God and missing the importance and value of honoring God's Word by remembering a day of rest. I mean, not only do we need it, but God commanded it! Stress, anxiety, depression, the weight of the world on your shoulders—those are real things. And I know that you, who are reading this right now, have been experiencing one of or all those at some level in your life. We all do.

We need a day to lay all that junk, that heavy weight we carry all week long, at the throne of God and to say, "God, I just need Your peace today. I want and need to hear from You today." It can get so easy for us, in the middle of all we have going on, to forget that He is our Shepherd and it's His job to carry *our* weight. We forget, so we try to carry it all, and it ends up crushing us. We desperately need a day of rest where we stop and remember to give it back to Him so that He can carry it all for us.

"OK, Kelly, I think I got it now. So that means on the Sabbath, I don't do anything. I just sit at my house and hang out with God." Let's think about this for a minute. Thinking this way turns the Sabbath into a law again. Your Sabbath, your day off, your day of rest—you can spend it anyway you want! You can spend it with your family, or you can spend it with your friends. If your wife's car breaks down, you can go fix it. If your friends want to go for a motorcycle ride, you can go. The point is to honor God with a day of rest. God's gift of the Sabbath to you is a day of relaxation and enjoyment because God knows you need it!

Look, if you want to go to church on Saturday, go on Saturday. If you want to go to church on Sunday, go on Sunday. Go any day you want. And if that's your day of rest too, awesome! Don't forget—the Sabbath was created as a gift to you from God. The truth is, God wants to spend twenty-four hours a day with you. But we make it seem like that is the biggest chore in the world. And He *knew* we would do that, so He gave us a gift, the Sabbath. This gift is designed to make it *easy* for us to spend time with Him. I think it's time we start using this gift and honoring the Lord with a day of rest—not turning it into another rule or law we have to try and follow, beating ourselves up when we miss it. We already have enough of that, don't you think?

Think of it like this: If I bought you a brand-new phone and gave it to you under the stipulation that you could use it six days a week but not on Saturdays, was that really a gift? Or was it a burden? When someone truly gives you a gift, you're the one who gets to choose how, when, and where you use it. You just need to make sure you use it!

Stop thinking of the Sabbath as simply "the day I go to church." Start thinking of it as one of the greatest gifts God ever gave you. A gift to take a day off. A day off from stress, worry, and anxiety. Use that gift to get yourself recentered on His Word. Use it to have fun with your friends and family. And if that's the same day you go to church, awesome. And if it's not, awesome. Don't fall into the trap of turning a gift from God into a law or rule. Gifts are made to be enjoyed, so go out and enjoy your Sabbath!

CHAPTER 19

What Is the Unforgivable Sin?

HAVE YOU EVER found yourself asking, or being asked by someone else, "Is there a sin that's too big to come back from? Is there such a thing as an unforgivable sin?" Right from the get-go, I know you may be jumping to a quick answer, thinking, "Jesus paid for all sins. Once you believe in Him, there is no sin too great." And that's understandable because the gospel teaches that grace covers us. But you may be saying, "Wait a second. No way! The Bible clearly says murderers won't inherit the kingdom of God. Adulterers are out too. And surely the 'rainbow community' won't be welcome either, right? I mean, that's what the Bible says—I think."

But here's the real question we should be asking: What does the Bible actually say? I am so glad we brought this up, because it's not just a question of opinions, assumptions, or what we think the Bible says. Let's dive into the Word and see what it truly reveals about this issue.

The Bible does indeed mention one sin that is deemed unforgivable, and I can promise you it's probably not the one you may expect or want it to be. Let's look at Matthew 12:31, where Jesus Himself says, "So I tell you, every sin and blasphemy can be forgiven—except blasphemy against the Holy Spirit, which will never be forgiven" (NLT). Yes, that's Jesus talking, straight from His own mouth. And just in case we missed it, He emphasizes again in the next verse, "Anyone who speaks against the Holy Spirit will not be forgiven, either in this age or in the age to come."

Whoa. That's heavy. Really heavy.

Now, hold on for a second. I can already imagine that you could be starting to panic a bit. Maybe you're thinking, "Oh my goodness—what if I've done this? I've said terrible things about Jesus. I've denied God's existence before. I've even said awful, horrible things about the Holy Spirit! Does this mean I'm not forgiven? Have I committed the unforgivable sin?" And if that's where your mind is going right now, please take a deep breath, and know that you're not alone. I had these exact same thoughts when I first came across these scriptures years ago, and they terrified me. But stick with me here because I'm going to try to bring some peace to your mind, just as the Holy Spirit did for me when I wrestled with this.

To truly understand what Jesus means when He talks about this unforgivable sin, we need to take a step back and look at the bigger picture. We need to ask, "Why did Jesus say this in the first place? What was happening at that moment?"

So here's the scene: Right before Jesus makes this

statement, a man is brought to Him. This man is both blind and unable to speak. On top of that, he is possessed by a demon. Jesus, being who He is, does what only He can do. He heals the man and casts out the demon. The man can both see and speak and is now free from the demonic oppression. It is a powerful moment. But standing nearby are the Pharisees, watching everything. Instead of acknowledging the miracle for what it is, a clear work of God, they make the shocking accusation that Jesus is able to do these things only because He is working in partnership with Satan.

Yes, you read that correctly. The Pharisees, the religious leaders of the day, claim that Jesus was empowered by the devil himself. It sounds absurd, doesn't it? But that's what they say. Jesus responds by essentially saying, "That doesn't even make sense. Satan may be evil, but he's not stupid! A kingdom divided against itself cannot stand." (See Matthew 12:22–28.) In other words, why would Satan cast out his own demons? It would be a self-defeating move, and even Satan isn't foolish enough to destroy his own work.

Then Jesus says something profound in Matthew 12:29. "Who is powerful enough to enter the house of a strong man and plunder his goods? Only someone even stronger—someone who could tie him up and then plunder his house" (NLT). What is Jesus saying here? He's making an important point: Satan is the *strong man*, and his *house* is this present world. His *goods* are the people he keeps in bondage, trapped in sin and darkness. But here's the good news: Jesus is the stronger One! Jesus has come to plunder Satan's house by rescuing the men and women who are trapped under his power.

Isn't that powerful? Think about it! Jesus is essentially saying, "I'm here to set people free! I have authority over the enemy!" But the Pharisees, despite witnessing this incredible miracle firsthand, choose to deny the work of the Holy Spirit. Instead, they attribute the power of God to Satan. That's where things take a serious turn.

In Mark 3:28–29 Jesus adds, "Truly I tell you, people can be forgiven all their sins and every slander they utter, but whoever blasphemes against the Holy Spirit will never be forgiven; they are guilty of an eternal sin." So here's the key point: All sins can be forgiven, with one exception—blasphemy against the Holy Spirit.

At this point you may be asking, "What was so bad about what the Pharisees did? Why was it unforgivable?" This is where we get to the heart of the issue.

Blasphemy against the Holy Spirit is not just a careless, onetime slipup. It's not a single outburst of anger or doubt. Instead, it's a deliberate, ongoing, and willful rejection of the work of the Holy Spirit. The Pharisees had just witnessed a miracle performed by Jesus through the power of the Holy Spirit. They saw it with their own eyes, yet they made the conscious choice to attribute that power to Satan. It wasn't a mistake or a misunderstanding; it was a defiant rejection of the truth they knew to be from God.

This wasn't just a onetime error in judgment for the Pharisees. It was a continuous, deliberate rebellion against God in the face of undeniable truth. That's what makes blasphemy against the Holy Spirit so dangerous. It's not something you do once out of anger and then feel remorse for. It's a hardened attitude of the heart, developed over time—a persistent rejection of the Holy Spirit's work.

And here's the kicker!

Jesus isn't saying that blasphemy will be forgiven *except* for blasphemy against the Holy Spirit. What He's saying is that any sin you genuinely repent of can be forgiven. But blasphemy against the Holy Spirit can never be forgiven, because it comes from a heart that is beyond repentance, a heart that is so hardened, it is incapable of turning back to God. And without repentance, there can be no forgiveness.

It's as simple as that.

You see, blasphemy against the Holy Spirit is a sin born out of complete indifference. It comes from a heart so calloused that it no longer cares. There's no conviction, no concern, no guilt—just a stubborn, willful rejection of the truth. And when someone reaches that point, they're beyond repentance and therefore beyond forgiveness. Jesus doesn't say this to scare us but to warn us.

If you're reading this and you're feeling a sense of worry, thinking, "Have I done this? Am I guilty of the unforgivable sin?" I have some good news for you. The very fact that you're concerned about it is all the proof you need that you haven't done it! If your heart is open, and if you still feel conviction, even just a little bit, then you haven't committed the unforgivable sin.

However, if you notice your heart becoming hard, or if

you find yourself rejecting the works of Jesus, doubting His power, and dismissing the miracles you see around you, be careful. That's dangerous ground. It's a slippery slope, and you don't want to go down that road.

"Yeah, but what if God hardens my heart? I mean, didn't He do that to Pharaoh?"

That's a great question. I'm glad you brought it up. God does harden Pharaoh's heart in the Book of Exodus, and it's easy to think, "Well, if God did it to Pharaoh, maybe He'll do it to me too." But let's take a closer look at what really happened.

Moses came to Pharaoh with many signs and wonders from God, miracles that were undeniable. Plague after plague, Pharaoh had the opportunity to see the power of the Holy Spirit at work. But instead of acknowledging the truth, Pharaoh chose to harden his own heart. He made a conscious decision to reject God's signs and wonders repeatedly. And as Pharaoh's heart grew harder, God finally affirmed the choice Pharaoh had already made. God didn't force Pharaoh's heart to harden against his will; Pharaoh made that decision himself, and God simply sealed it.

Here's what you need to know: God will never harden the heart of someone who hasn't already started hardening their heart on their own. If you're seeking God, if you're open to His conviction, and if you're willing to repent, you don't need to fear. Your heart is not beyond saving.

So let me encourage you today!

If you're reading this because you're worried that you've committed the unforgivable sin, take heart. The fact that you're even concerned about it shows that you haven't. If your heart is still soft, if you still feel the conviction of the Holy Spirit, you're in a good place. Keep that heart open to God's leading, and you'll never have to worry about committing the unforgivable sin.

If you love Jesus and have repented of your sins, meaning you've changed your mind and your direction, you are forgiven. You're not perfect; none of us are. But you're following His Word. Even if you've said terrible things about God in the past, even if you've cursed Jesus or spoken ill of the Holy Spirit, you are completely and totally forgiven. God looks at your heart, not your mistakes. Jesus already paid the price for those mistakes on the cross.

As long as you keep your heart open to repentance, this is not something you'll ever need to worry about. Walk in the freedom of knowing that Jesus has set you free and that His grace is more than enough for you.

Ultimately, the unforgivable sin isn't about an isolated act or mistake. It's about the condition of your heart. A heart that is humble, open, and repentant will always find forgiveness in Jesus. But a heart that chooses to reject the truth, no matter how obvious that truth is, is in danger of hardening to the point of no return. So keep your heart soft. Keep seeking God. And rest in the assurance that His grace is more than enough.

Jesus is stronger than the strongman, and He has come to set you free. Walk in that freedom today, knowing that as long as your heart is open to Him, you are fully and completely forgiven.

CHAPTER 20

Is Suicide a Ticket
Straight to Hell?

A QUESTION I'VE HEARD before, and one that weighs heavily on many hearts, is whether a Christian who takes their own life can still enter heaven. It's a difficult and emotional subject. Recently, a man shared with me that he had left his church because his father, who dearly loved Jesus, died by suicide. His pastor told him, "Your dad is 100 percent in hell, without a shadow of a doubt, because that's what the Bible says."

Wow.

First off, if you've ever heard something like that from someone who is supposed to be teaching you the Word of God, I want to tell you I am deeply sorry. Those words carry a lot of pain, and they may leave you questioning both your faith and the fate of your loved one. But let's slow down for a moment and take a look at what the Bible *actually* says. We need to dig deep into God's Word, with compassion and wisdom, to understand this sensitive issue.

Is suicide a sin?

Yes, it is.

The Bible says in Exodus 20:13, "You shall not commit murder" (AMP). Most are familiar with this commandment, and here's the thing: Suicide is considered a form of self-murder. God values life, and He created each of us with a purpose. In 1 Corinthians 3:17 Paul wrote, "If anyone destroys God's temple, God will destroy that person; for God's temple is sacred, and you together are that temple." Our bodies are the temples of the Holy Spirit, and we are called to care for them.

This is a tough pill to swallow, right? Because when someone takes their own life, it feels like they've stepped outside God's plan. They've acted out of deep despair or mental illness, and it leaves us grappling with the eternal consequences of their action. But suicide is *not* the unforgivable sin.

Let me explain.

Before you jump to any conclusions, let's take a step back and look at the bigger picture. When Jesus died on the cross, He paid for every sin—past, present, and future. That includes the sins we haven't even committed yet. First John 1:9 says, "If we confess our sins, He is faithful and just to forgive us our sins and to cleanse us from all unrighteousness" (NKJV).

Let's break that down.

When we give our hearts to Jesus and confess our sins, something miraculous happens. God, in His faithfulness, not only forgives us but also purifies us. That means the blood of Jesus covers all sin, every sin we've committed and every sin we will commit. Yes, even suicide.

I can hear the objection already.

"But Kelly, doesn't that mean people will just think they can live however they want and do whatever they want, since we're saved and all our sins are forgiven?"

No, that's not what I'm saying at all. Once you give your life to Jesus, it's not just about believing He exists. It's about allowing Him to take up residency in your life. But even more than that, Jesus doesn't just want residency; He wants presidency. He wants to be Lord over every aspect of your life.

That's why we're called to renew our minds constantly, as the Bible says in Romans 12:2, "Do not conform to the pattern of this world, but be transformed by the renewing of your mind." Life with Christ is a process. It's a journey of surrendering more and more to Him. And this journey doesn't exempt us from struggles with mental health, anxiety, or depression.

The sad reality is that there are many amazing men and women of God who love Jesus, serve Him, and live faithfully yet still lose the battle of depression. Depression is a disease, just like any other illness, and it affects the brain in profound ways. It can cloud judgment, distort reality, and make people feel trapped in a darkness they can't escape. So when someone takes their own life in a moment of despair, it's not because they didn't love God. And it's not because God stopped loving them.

Was suicide God's plan for them? No, of course not. Jeremiah 29:11 tells us that God has a plan for our lives— a plan to prosper us and not to harm us, a plan to give us hope and a future. Suicide cuts that plan short. But Romans 8:38–39 reminds us that nothing—not life, not death, not angels, not demons—can "separate us from the love of God that is in Christ Jesus our Lord." Even suicide cannot separate us from God's love.

Here's another question I hear quite often: "Kelly, you just said we need to repent for our sins. But if someone dies by suicide, how can they repent afterward?" I understand why this feels like a tricky issue, so let's break it down.

When we first come to Christ, we repent for salvation. That repentance is a turning away from our old lives and a choice to follow Jesus. In that moment, we receive the gift of salvation, freely given and fully paid for by Jesus' sacrifice on the cross. All our sins—past, present, and future—are covered by His blood.

However, after we're saved, we will continue to struggle with sin. This is why we repent again and again—not to earn salvation but to restore our relationship with God. At this point, it becomes repentance for restoration, not salvation. Think of it like this: When you're adopted into a family, your status as a son or daughter doesn't change when you make a mistake. Every time you mess up, you don't have to go down to the courthouse and have the judge put you back in the family. That would be ridiculous! You're still part of the family, but you might need to apologize to repair the relationship.

Salvation is not something we earn. Ephesians 2:8–9 tells us it is by grace we have been saved, through faith, not by works, so no one can boast. If salvation depended on our ability to be perfect, none of us would make it. But because salvation is a gift, we don't lose it when we fall short. We come to God in repentance not to be saved over and over again but to maintain the closeness of our relationship with Him.

So does the act of suicide cancel out a lifetime of faith in Jesus? No, it doesn't. The grace of God is bigger than our moments of failure.

Now, some people may point to the Bible and say, "But isn't there an unforgivable sin?" Yes, the Bible does mention one sin that cannot be forgiven: blasphemy of the Holy Spirit. This sin is essentially a hardened, deliberate rejection of the Holy Spirit's work and the salvation Jesus offers.

The person who commits this sin is someone whose heart has become so hardened toward God that they have no desire to repent. They have completely rejected the gift of salvation, and that's why it's unforgivable, because they have turned away from the only One who can save them. It's not because God's grace isn't big enough to cover it but because that grace is rejected by them entirely. (See chapter 19 in this book for a discussion of the unforgivable sin.)

Let's return to a hypothetical example. Suppose a Christian man with a deep personal relationship with the Lord is driving home from work. As he drives, he sees a beautiful woman walking along the sidewalk and finds himself staring. In that moment, he begins to lust after her. Distracted by his thoughts, he misses the red light and ends up in a fatal car accident. He didn't have time to repent of his lustful thoughts. So does that mean he's condemned to hell?

Of course not.

God's grace doesn't hinge on whether we can repent of every sin in every single moment. The key here is that this man had already repented for salvation. His relationship with Jesus was secure, and his eternity wasn't determined by one fleeting moment of sin. The same is true for those who die by suicide. If they have placed their faith in Jesus, their eternity is secure, even if their life ends tragically.

If you have lost someone to suicide and you know they loved Jesus, I want to encourage you today. I fully believe you will see them again in eternity. God's grace is sufficient, and His love covers all. Jesus paid for it all, and nothing can snatch us out of His hands.

If you're struggling with thoughts of self-harm or suicide, please know that this is not the end of your story. God sees you. He loves you more than you could ever comprehend. He has a plan for your life, and no matter how dark things may seem right now, there is hope for you. Don't believe the lies of the enemy, who wants to rob you of the future God has planned for you.

You are fearfully and wonderfully made. You are not a mistake; you are a masterpiece. You are deeply loved by the One who created you.

If you need someone to talk to right now, please reach out. Text D2L to 91627, and someone from the Death2Life ministry will be there to speak with you. You don't have to go through this alone. There is hope, and there is help.

CHAPTER 21

Can a Christian Be Cremated?

W HEN THINKING ABOUT the final resting place of our physical bodies, a question that has come up often in Christian circles is whether a person who has been cremated can still enter heaven. If you've ever asked yourself or heard this question, you're not alone. In fact, when I initially mentioned the idea of writing this book to my followers online, I didn't plan to address cremation. However, the overwhelming responses and requests from people made it clear that this topic needed to be included. So for you all who tune in to my morning live Bible studies, this one is dedicated to you. Let's dive into what the Bible has to say on this issue and unravel the confusion surrounding cremation.

If you've ever heard the saying "When Jesus comes back, our bodies will rise to meet Him in the air," it may have led you to wonder, "What happens if my body is cremated? There wouldn't be anything left to rise, so does that mean I can't be part of the resurrection?"

This line of thinking can cause anxiety, leading

people to question their futures with Christ. However, let me put your mind at ease right from the start.

The Bible neither explicitly condones nor condemns cremation.

Cremation as a practice is mentioned in Scripture but often in less-than-ideal situations. Let's examine these examples closely to get a better understanding.

For example, consider the story of Achan, who disobeyed God's command during the time of the Israelite conquest of Jericho. A soldier, Achan was part of the team that entered Jericho after the walls fell, and God gave a clear instruction that nothing from the city was to be taken as a spoil. However, Achan secretly decided to keep some of the goods for himself. When Joshua, the leader of the Israelites, asked the people who had taken what was forbidden, Achan remained silent, refusing to confess. His dishonesty led to severe consequences. Once it was revealed that Achan had taken forbidden items, not only was he stoned to death along with his family, but their bodies were burned afterward as part of the punishment. (See Joshua 7.)

In this case cremation followed as a result of God's judgment on Achan's disobedience. It's a sobering story, and one might initially conclude that cremation is associated with only punishment and disgrace.

However, there's another example that presents a different side to cremation. In the Book of 1 Samuel we read about the tragic end of King Saul and his sons, who were killed in battle. Their bodies were mutilated by the Philistines as a form of ridicule. In an effort to protect them from further desecration, the people burned their bodies and then buried their bones. (See 1 Samuel 31.) This instance of burning the bodies wasn't about punishment—it was done out of respect and care for the deceased, to protect them from enemy humiliation.

These two stories show us that cremation in the Bible appears in both negative and neutral contexts. In one it was part of a punishment, and in another it was a practical and respectful choice. So based on these examples alone, we can see that cremation isn't inherently sinful or forbidden.

Most of the debate about cremation centers on passages that describe the resurrection of the dead. The most commonly cited passage is from 1 Corinthians 15, where the apostle Paul discusses the resurrection. Specifically, verse 42 says, "So will it be with the resurrection of the dead. The body that is sown is perishable, it is raised imperishable." At first glance it may seem as if Paul is saying that a body must be buried (*sown*) in order to be raised. And naturally, if one is cremated, there's no body left to be *sown* into the ground. This leads many to argue that cremation prevents resurrection.

But let's take a closer look.

The key to understanding Paul's teaching on resurrection is realizing that he's drawn a distinction between our earthly bodies and our resurrected bodies. In the same chapter, Paul wrote, "But someone will ask, 'How are the dead raised? With what kind of body will they come?' How foolish! What you sow does not come to life unless it dies" (vv. 35–36). Paul used the analogy of planting a seed. When you plant a seed in the ground, the plant that emerges doesn't look anything like the seed. It's transformed. In the same way, when our physical bodies die, they aren't the same bodies that will be raised in the resurrection.

Paul made it clear that our resurrected bodies are not the same as our earthly ones. In fact, our earthly bodies are described as perishable, weak, and dishonorable compared with the glorious, imperishable, powerful, and spiritual bodies we will receive in the resurrection. When a seed is planted, it dies in the sense that it undergoes a transformation. Similarly, our earthly bodies will undergo a transformation to become something entirely new in the resurrection.

Therefore, the concern about whether a cremated body can be resurrected is misplaced. The Bible never claims that the same physical body that was buried will rise again. Instead, it emphasizes the transformation from a perishable to an imperishable state. Whether your body is buried intact or cremated, or even lost at sea, it is God's power that will give you a new, glorified body at the resurrection.

If you may still have lingering doubts, let me pose a question. Have you ever considered what happens to a body that has been buried for a long period of time? Over time buried bodies decompose and turn into dust. Even in cases of traditional burial, the physical body eventually disintegrates, becoming indistinguishable from the soil around it. Cremation simply accelerates this process, reducing the body to ashes much more quickly. If we accept that God can resurrect a body that has decomposed over centuries, surely He can also resurrect a body that has been cremated.

The truth is that these physical bodies, or what I like to call our flesh suits, are temporary. They serve us while we are here on earth, but they are not designed to last forever. Our eternal existence will not be limited by the conditions of our earthly bodies. God, who created the heavens and the earth, is certainly powerful enough to give us new, perfect bodies in the resurrection, no matter what state our earthly bodies are in when we die.

Think of the many Christians throughout history who have died in circumstances where their bodies were destroyed—whether by fire, war, natural disasters, or other tragic events. Are we to believe that God cannot resurrect them because their bodies are not intact? Of course not! God is not limited by the physical conditions of our earthly remains. His power transcends all earthly limitations.

One of the most powerful truths of the Christian faith is that Jesus' tomb is empty. After His crucifixion, Jesus' body was placed in a tomb, but on the third day He rose from the dead. His resurrection is the cornerstone of our faith, and it assures us that we too will rise. But when Jesus rose, He didn't return in the same beaten and broken body that had been laid in the tomb. He was given a glorified body, one that could appear and disappear, one that still bore the scars of the crucifixion but was no longer subject to pain, death, or decay.

This same promise applies to us. Whether our earthly

bodies are buried, cremated, or lost, we will receive new, glorified bodies in the resurrection. Jesus' resurrection demonstrates God's power over death and decay, and it guarantees that we too will experience the same transformation.

So can a Christian's body be cremated and still get into heaven? Absolutely. The Bible does not prohibit cremation, and God's ability to resurrect us is not limited by the state of our earthly remains. Whether we are buried or cremated, what matters most is our relationship with Jesus Christ.

If you have accepted Jesus as your Lord and Savior, you can rest assured that your future is secure. When Christ returns, He will give you a new, glorified body that is free from pain, sickness, and death. Our earthly bodies are just temporary vessels, and once we are done with this life, we will leave them behind and step into something far greater.

Don't live in fear or uncertainty. If you or your loved ones have chosen cremation, know that it will not prevent you all from participating in the resurrection. As Christians our hope is not in our earthly bodies but in the promise of eternal life with Christ. And that, my friend, is truly good news!

CHAPTER 22

Did Judas Go to Hell?

WHEN I TEACH online, my comment sections fill up pretty fast. Most of the time it's encouragement. Sometimes it's hateful, but every once in a while, I see some truly amazing questions. The topic we are about to explore comes straight from one of those questions.

"Did Judas go to hell? Doesn't suicide mean instant hell? Judas knew he was in the wrong, so is there any chance at all that he made it to heaven?"

What a phenomenal question! And you know what? The Bible does provide us with some insight on this topic. However, if I were to say flippantly, "Yes, he went to hell," or, "No, he didn't," that would likely raise even more questions than it would answer. There's much more to this topic, and we're going to dive deep into it. Let's take a look at the Bible and see what it has to say about Judas, his actions, and his eternal destiny.

First, let's get real for a second. A person's eternal destiny is ultimately up to God. We, as humans, simply can't say with absolute certainty where anyone ends up when they die. That's because only God truly knows the condition of their heart. Only He knows the totality of their choices and motivations and whether they sought forgiveness in their final moments. That being said, there is some pretty strong evidence from Jesus' own words that suggests Judas *did* end up in hell.

Let me show you.

In Matthew 26:24, during the last supper, Jesus says, "For the Son of Man must die, as the Scriptures declared long ago. But how terrible it will be for the one who betrays him. It would be far better for that man if he had never been born!" (NLT). Now, pause and think about that statement. In the words of Marty McFly from *Back to the Future*, "Whoa. This is heavy." Jesus was saying that the outcome for the man (Judas) who was about to betray Him would be so severe, so tragic, that he would wish he had never been born. That's a chilling statement. I've had lots of people make threats to me over my lifetime, saying, "You'll wish you had never been born"—my mother probably being the one who has used that the most! But to hear those words coming from the lips of Jesus?

Whoa. That cuts deep.

Jesus isn't one to throw around casual statements, especially not about matters of eternal consequence. When He speaks of someone's eternal fate with that kind of gravity, we need to take it seriously. His words suggest that Judas' betrayal carried with it a weight so heavy, a punishment so severe, that nonexistence would be preferable to what awaited him. And that's a huge clue about Judas' fate.

But there's more.

In John 17:12, while Jesus is praying, He says, "During my time here, I protected them by the power of the name you gave me. I guarded them so that not one was lost, except the one headed for destruction, as the Scriptures foretold" (NLT). Take a moment to digest this. Jesus is specifically saying that one of His disciples *is* "headed for destruction"—not that "he might be if he doesn't change his ways" and not "possibly, if he fails to repent." Jesus says that he is already on the road to destruction, and it's foretold in the Scriptures. This isn't a casual statement. It's a declaration of a tragic destiny that, according to Jesus, Judas is already on.

This verse brings up another interesting question, though, doesn't it?

"Did God force Judas to betray Jesus so that the Scriptures could be fulfilled? Because that doesn't sound like the loving God I know."

That is an excellent question, and it's one we will explore a bit further in just a minute.

But based on these two scriptures alone and the very clear and direct statements made by Jesus Himself, it appears that Judas' fate was indeed one of eternal separation from God. His betrayal wasn't just a political or social misstep; it was a betrayal of the very Son of God. And as Jesus warned, the consequences for such an act would be grave.

But here's where things get even more interesting.

Some will ask, "Did Judas go to hell because he committed suicide? Isn't that the unforgivable sin?"

This is where a lot of confusion can arise, and I want to be crystal clear on this point. No, Judas didn't go to hell because he committed suicide. Suicide in and of itself isn't what condemned him. (Chapter 20 of this book covers the topic of suicide and what the Bible says about it.) The reason Judas went to hell, based on Scripture, is that he didn't repent. He realized the gravity of what he had done, but instead of turning back to Jesus for forgiveness and restoration, he chose to end his life.

And here's the takeaway: Feeling bad about your sin isn't the same as repenting from your sin and seeking forgiveness.

This is where the story of Judas intersects with the story of Peter, and the contrast between the two is incredibly important. Let's take a moment to compare Judas and Peter. Both of them messed up big-time. Judas betrayed Jesus, which led to His arrest and crucifixion. Peter, on the other hand, denied Jesus three times even though he had sworn he never would. Both were disloyal in critical moments.

However, there's a key difference between them: Peter came back. He repented. He sought forgiveness. And because of that he was forgiven and restored by Jesus. Judas, tragically, did not. That's the crucial difference. It's not about how badly you've sinned; it's about whether you turn back to Jesus afterward.

In John 17:12 (ESV) when Jesus refers to Judas as "the

son of destruction," He's indicating that Judas had chosen a path that led to eternal separation from God, not because of the betrayal alone, and not because of the suicide, but because Judas didn't seek the forgiveness that Jesus so freely offers.

So let's circle back to that earlier question: Did God force Judas to betray Jesus so that the Scriptures could be fulfilled?

The answer, again, is no. God doesn't force anyone to sin. God doesn't make us sin so that His plans can unfold. That's not how God operates. He doesn't need to coerce anyone into wrongdoing. God knew what Judas was going to do, before He created the world. He knew that Judas would betray Jesus, and He knew that Judas, despite the gravity of his sin, would choose not to repent. God, in His foreknowledge, incorporated Judas' decision into His ultimate plan for redemption.

There's a big difference between foreknowledge and predestination, and this is where a lot of people get tripped up. *Predestination* is the idea that God has already decided what will happen, and no one can change it. *Foreknowledge*, on the other hand, is God's ability to know what will happen before it does, without forcing anyone to make particular choices.

A great example of this distinction can be found in 1 Samuel 23:10–12 (NLT). Here, we see David getting word that King Saul was planning to come and kill him and his men. David, being the wise leader he was, sought guidance from God.

> Then David prayed, "O LORD, God of Israel, I have heard that Saul is planning to come and destroy Keilah because I am here. Will the leaders of Keilah betray me to him? And will Saul actually come as I have heard? O LORD, God of Israel, please tell me." And the LORD said, "He will come." Again David asked, "Will the leaders of Keilah betray me and my men to Saul?" And the LORD replied, "Yes, they will betray you."

David got his answer! Saul was coming, and the leaders of Keilah were going to betray David. Yet despite this forewarning Saul never actually came. Wait—what? Did God lie to David?

Absolutely not! God knew Saul's intentions. In Saul's heart he fully intended to come after David and destroy Keilah. But since God told David what was going to happen, David left Keilah, and Saul never got the chance to attack. God didn't predestine Saul's attack. He merely knew Saul's plan ahead of time and warned David. In this way God's foreknowledge allowed David to make a decision that altered the outcome. God always knows what we will choose, but He doesn't force our choices.

Likewise, God didn't force Judas to betray Jesus. Judas made that choice of his own free will. God, in His infinite wisdom, simply incorporated Judas' decision into His larger plan for salvation. Judas hardened his own heart. God didn't harden it for him.

The bottom line is this: Judas went to hell because he didn't repent, not because he committed suicide. His sin of betrayal was grave, but Judas' refusal to seek forgiveness was what ultimately sealed his fate. And as for suicide? It's not an automatic ticket to hell. There's so much more to God's grace and forgiveness than we often give Him credit for.

Here's the thing: Jesus offers us something far better than despair, far better than hopelessness. He offers eternal life, hope, and a future. So no matter what you're going through, run to Him. Nothing you have done is so terrible that you can't repent and turn back to Jesus. Let Judas be a sobering example of what happens when we choose not to seek that forgiveness. Yes, sin separates us from God, but repentance brings us back to fellowship with Him. Repentance is the key that unlocks restoration.

Judas' story is tragic, but it serves as a powerful reminder. Even when we make mistakes, even when we fall into sin, there's always a path back to God if we're willing to repent and seek forgiveness. Judas' downfall wasn't predestined or forced upon him. It was a result of his own choices—choices he never sought to undo by turning back to Jesus. Let's let his story remind us that no matter how far we fall, Jesus is always ready to forgive, restore, and welcome us back into His arms.

CHAPTER 23

Are Aliens Real?

RECENTLY, I WAS asked on one of my social media platforms, "Did God create aliens? The government is coming forward with stunning evidence of UFOs. Does the Bible talk about this?"

I can definitely see how this would cause fear in some people. "Are we in the last days? Did God actually create aliens? Is this all a ruse from our government?" I know, I know, there are a million conspiracy theories floating around out there. But I don't care about theories; I care about the Word of God. The truth is, this shouldn't scare us at all.

You may be thinking, "Great. As if we didn't have enough in our world to worry about, now we have to add aliens to the list as well!" If that's you, let me try to bring some peace to your mind today.

"So what does the Bible say about all this?"

I'm so glad you asked! If you look in Matthew 24 in the New Living Translation, in verses 4–5 Jesus tells His disciples, "Don't let anyone mislead you, for many will come in my name, claiming, 'I am the Messiah.' They will deceive many."

Jesus Himself said that things like this were going to happen. Many will come to try to deceive us and claim to be Jesus or God. But when the scripture says that "they will deceive many," the question we need to answer first is, Who are the *many*? For me, growing up in church, I always thought this meant sinners. You know, the lost. Worldly people. Because, us Christians? We're not going to be deceived! We know who Jesus is.

Don't we?

To find out exactly who this is talking about, we need to read forward a little. In Matthew 24:12–13 Jesus paints a clear picture of what the end times will look like. He says, "Sin will be rampant everywhere [does that sound like anyplace you know right now?], and the love of many will grow cold. But the one who endures to the end will be saved" (NLT). Pay attention; we see another group of *many* here. It's important to note that this is the same group as the *many* who will be deceived.

OK, let's break this down.

We can all agree that sin is rampant everywhere right now. Never before in our cultures, our countries, and our world has the love of sin been so strong and so completely out in the open. It's as if the devil isn't even trying to hide anymore. And the world appears to be just fine with that. "Yeah, Kelly, but not for us Christians. You can't fool us, devil!"

OK, OK. But watch this. The scripture says, "The love of *many* will grow cold" (emphasis added). And this is the same *many* that will be deceived, remember? So let's get back to our question: Who are the *many*?

To get the correct answer, we need to look at the word *love* used here in this verse. Now, in the Bible, we have four Greek words that are used for *love*. There is *philia*, which describes the type of love found in strong friendships. Then you have *eros*. This is more of an erotic love that you would find in a romantic relationship. Next is *storge*, a family type of love, like you would have for a brother or sister. And then lastly is *agape*, the greatest love of them all. *Agape* is selfless and unconditional. This is the love of God. Anyone can experience the first three loves we discussed, whether they are saved or not. However, *agape* is only for those in a personal relationship with Jesus Christ.

You see, God doesn't have love; God *is* love. That's *agape*! Until you have God in your life by accepting Jesus as your Lord and Savior, you have not experienced and will not experience this type of love. So when our verse says, "The love of many will grow cold," which one does it use? It uses *agape*! The *many* that this verse is talking about here is Christians! It's people who have experienced the deep, perfect, selfless, endless love of God.

"Nah, Kelly, I don't know if I believe that, man. You're not gonna get us Christians so easily." Well, I hear what you're saying, but the next line in the verse proves exactly what I'm saying: "The one who endures to the end will be saved" (v. 13, NLT). Hebrews 12:1 tells us to run the race set before us with endurance. The

Bible compares our journey with God to being in a race. You can't endure to the end of the race if you have never even started the race!

Please don't miss this. This is absolutely talking about believers. But here's the thing: My whole life, growing up in church, when I would hear this preached as "somebody's coming, and they're going to try to deceive us and turn us away from Jesus," I always pictured some guy showing up and claiming to be Jesus. I pictured him doing miraculous signs and wonders, and I could see how people would be easily deceived by that. But now that I'm older and a bit wiser, I don't believe that's going to be the case anymore.

Back in biblical times, if some dude showed up doing all sorts of miracles and claiming to be God, they would absolutely be easily deceived. But not us today. As it stands right now, we have an explanation for *everything*. If that happened today, we would write it off as an illusion, some sort of magic trick. That's when this thought hit me: What would it actually take to deceive *many* Christians? It would take something huge that would seemingly be unexplainable, something we'd think we couldn't find in the Word of God. You following me yet? It would have to take something like, oh, I don't know, massive technology. Perhaps a "life form" other than what we see in the Bible. You got it.

Aliens.

Let's be honest. New believers or Christians who are weak in their faith would have no way to explain that. They wouldn't know what scripture to stand on. Not to mention, the devil has been programming us for years. Please understand, the devil doesn't attack *Mad Max* style, all guns blazing. Our enemy's agenda is destruction, and his plan is division. And, my friend, he is more patient than you or I ever could be. He has no problem attacking little by little by little. He has been putting ideas into our minds through movies, TV shows, books, music—everything—so that when the time comes, we've already been looking for him! But so many won't know or be able to tell that it's actually the work of Satan.

"So, Kelly, you're telling me aliens actually *do* exist? Do you believe this?"

Let me make this part loud and clear.

No! I do *not* believe in aliens. But I do believe in *demons*.

Understand—the devil hates you, and he will do anything he can to steal, kill, and destroy you and the plan God has spoken over your life. The truth is, he knows we're all looking for something greater than ourselves. And if our foundation in Jesus isn't solid and our faith is based on what our eyes see and our ears hear instead of the truth found in God's Word, aliens may sound like a pretty good plan to deceive *many*.

Who knows, we may see some aliens showing up pretty soon, and they may do some amazing things. Do not be deceived! Matthew 24:26–27 says, "So if someone tells you, 'Look, the Messiah is out in the desert,' don't bother to go and look. [Where is Area 51 again? Oh yeah, the desert.] Or, 'Look, he is hiding [conspiracy theories and government cover-ups] here,' don't believe it! For as the lightning flashes in the east and shines to the west, so it will be when the Son of Man comes" (NLT). Jesus is telling you that no matter what people say, no matter what it may look like, *don't be deceived*!

If some little green dude shows up and starts raising people from the dead, it ain't Jesus!

It breaks my heart to think the *agape* love of so many is going to grow cold. But because we have the Word of God, we've always known it is going to happen—it just doesn't have to be me or you, though.

So let me encourage you today. Is this the end of the world? Are we in the last days? Honestly, it really doesn't matter. Jesus has already overcome this world, and if you have the Holy Spirit living inside you, and if you are walking close with Jesus, you don't have to live in fear.

"Yeah, Kelly, but this world is a *dark* place right now. It's just so dark!"

To that I say, "Yes, and I love that!"

"Uh, what? How could you be a Jesus follower and love that the world is so dark?"

I'll tell you how.

Jesus is the Light of the world. And since you have Jesus in you, Matthew 5:14 says that "you are the light of the world" (NLT). Let me ask you a question. Where does light do its best work? In the darkness!

Yes, the world may be a dark place right now. Thanks, devil—you just made my job easy! Stop living in fear of what *may* come. Or what could *possibly* happen. We knew this was going to happen. We read it over and over again in our Bibles. Your job is to go out and be a light in the darkness. The whole world is looking for an answer right now. And we have it!

If the devil can shut you up and get you to stop shining your light, he wins. So I say we don't let him. Come what may, our hope and faith are in Jesus alone. Let's keep building our foundation on Him. Let's endure to the end. Aliens or no aliens, it changes *nothing* for a true believer in Jesus Christ!

CHAPTER 24

Is It a Sin for Christians to Drink Alcohol or Smoke Cigarettes?

THE QUESTION OF whether smoking or drinking alcohol is a sin is one of the most common questions I receive on a daily basis. No matter how many times I address this question, it comes up again and again. And that's OK because it reflects a genuine concern among believers who are trying to understand how their faith intersects with their actions. However, let me start by saying that the principles I'm about to share with you here apply to much more than just smoking or drinking. These ideas can be applied to just about *anything* in your life as a Christian. Even if you don't smoke or drink, I encourage you to keep reading, as you may discover something valuable that can help you in your walk with God.

First and foremost, we need to recognize that this is what I would call a milk question, a basic or foundational question in your walk with God. It's the type of question a person may ask when they are new to the faith or early in their spiritual journey, because they're trying to figure out what is acceptable in the eyes of God. That's perfectly normal and expected. However, if you've been a follower of Jesus for a significant amount of time and are still wrestling with this question, or questions like it, it may indicate you need to take a closer look at your understanding of God's grace and mercy. These two concepts, grace and mercy, are critical for any believer to grasp fully because they form the foundation of how we live out our faith.

Let's break this down and look at what *mercy* and *grace* mean for us as believers.

Mercy is when you don't receive the punishment you rightfully deserve. According to the Bible, every single one of us deserves eternal separation from God. That's a sobering thought, and some may even think it's a bit harsh. But Scripture is clear: "For all have sinned and fall short of the glory of God" (Rom. 3:23). That means we are all guilty before God, and the penalty for sin is death. However, when Jesus Christ died on the cross for us, He took that punishment upon Himself. This act was the ultimate display of mercy because it spared us from the eternal consequences of our sins. On the other hand, *grace* is the unmerited favor of God. *Grace* is when God gives us blessings we didn't earn and certainly don't deserve.

Let me paint a mental picture for you of what these actually look like.

Imagine you're driving 90 miles per hour in a 65 mph

zone, and you get pulled over by a police officer. At that moment, you know you're guilty and deserve a ticket. But instead of writing you a ticket, the officer lets you off with a warning. "Oh, thank God the officer showed me grace!" Um, no, he didn't. That's mercy. You were spared the punishment you deserved. Now imagine that the officer not only lets you go without a ticket but also hands you $1,000 in cash and wishes you a blessed day. That's grace! You were in the wrong, you were guilty, you didn't deserve the gift, but you received it anyway. This is how God's mercy and grace work in our lives.

So what does this have to do with smoking and drinking? Well, it's important to understand that when Jesus died on the cross, He paid the price for all our sins—past, present, and future. This includes sins related to substances such as alcohol or tobacco. We have already mentioned this several times in this book, and I hope you're catching on to the trend, but here we go again! In 1 Corinthians 6:12, the apostle Paul wrote, "All things are permitted for me" (NRSVUE). In other words, we are no longer under the Old Testament Law, and we don't have to live in constant fear of committing a sin that will separate us from God. Jesus has already taken care of that. However, Paul also adds, "but not all things are beneficial" (v. 12, NRSVUE). Just because something is permissible doesn't mean it's good for you or that it will help you grow closer to God.

When it comes to smoking and drinking, the question kind of answers itself, doesn't it? I mean, is there any way possible to say these activities benefit your life?

In fact, they do the exact opposite. Think about it like this: God has a call and plan for your life. For all our lives. And in that plan there lies a number—a number of souls you are responsible to share the gospel with. Now, smoking and drinking may not send you to hell, but they can drastically shorten your life. The shorter your life, the less time you have to reach the people God intended you to reach. And if your life ends before its appointed time because you chose to smoke and drink instead of honoring the Lord with your body, you will have missed out on part of the call and plan God has for you. Is this starting to click yet?

What I'm trying to show you is that the bigger issue here isn't necessarily about whether something is sinful in a technical sense. The real question is whether the things we choose to do bring us closer to God or pull us further away. It's easy to get caught up in a checklist mentality where we focus on whether certain actions will send us to hell or if we can get away with them and still make it to heaven.

But that's missing the point.

Our goal as Christians should not be to see how close we can get to sin without crossing the line. Instead, our goal should be to get as close to God as possible, to seek Him with our whole hearts, and to align our lives with His will.

When we ask, "Is smoking or drinking a sin?" what we're really asking is, "How far can I push the boundaries and still be OK?" But the better questions to ask are, "Does this bring me closer to God? Can this activity be used to glorify God or lead others to Him?" If the answer is no, then it's time to reevaluate whether it's something we should be doing.

God cares more about the conditions of our hearts than anything else. In Matthew 15:11 Jesus says, "It is not what goes into the mouth that defiles a person, but it is what comes out of the mouth that defiles" (NRSVUE). This means our external actions are not the primary issue. Instead, God is concerned with our motives and what's going on inside our hearts. If smoking or drinking or any other behavior comes from a place of trying to escape, numb pain, or fill a void that only God can fill, then it's time to address that deeper issue.

Now, let me clarify something.

Even after you give your life to Jesus, you're still going to mess up. You're still going to sin. I know we have talked about that before, but the best way to get something from your head to your heart is through repetition.

Some people believe it's possible to live a completely sin-free life once you've been saved, but that's not what the Bible teaches. The reality is that we are all made up of three parts: body, soul, and spirit. Your spirit was made perfect the moment you accepted Jesus as your Lord and Savior. It's your spirit that craves God and desires to do His will. However, your body (your flesh) still craves sin. That's why even after becoming a Christian, you still struggle with temptation. The good news is that your flesh doesn't have to have the final say!

Your soul, which consists of your mind, will, and emotions, is the battleground. You have to make a conscious decision, multiple times a day, to align your mind, will, and emotions with your spirit rather than your flesh. When you do that with the help of the Holy Spirit, you'll find the strength to resist temptation and overcome the sinful desires of the flesh.

"OK, but what does this look like in real life? How do we do that, Kelly?"

Well, instead of constantly worrying about whether something is a sin, start asking different questions. Ask yourself, "Is this bringing me closer to God? Is this something that Jesus would do? Would I feel comfortable doing this if I knew the Holy Spirit was right here with me?" (News flash: He is!) These are the kinds of questions that will keep you focused on growing in your relationship with God rather than getting bogged down in legalism or guilt.

Remember, whatever you focus on will become magnified in your life. If you focus on God and His goodness, He will become the most prominent thing in your life. But if you focus on sin and your failures, then those will become the biggest things in your life. That's why it's so important to fix your eyes on Jesus and let Him guide your steps. When you're close to Him, the things of this world, including the temptations and distractions, will start to lose their appeal.

So let me encourage you today!

Let's stop asking, "Is _____ a sin?" and start asking, "Is this helping me become more like Christ?" Let's strive to live lives that honor God and reflect His love and grace to the world around us. Smoking and drinking may not be the biggest issues at hand. The more significant question is whether our actions are helping us grow closer to the One who gave everything for us. So before you make any decision, take a moment to reflect on your heart and motives. Ask God for guidance, and He will lead you in the right direction.

Ultimately, it's not about following a set of rules. It's about cultivating a relationship with the living God. He desires to be close to you, to walk with you through every area of your life, and to help you make decisions that will bring you joy, peace, and fulfillment. So the next time you're faced with a decision, whether it's about smoking or drinking, or anything else, ask yourself, Will this help me get closer to God? And if the answer is no, then you already know what to do. Choose Him every time, and watch how your life transforms in ways you never thought possible.

CHAPTER 25

What Will Eternity Be Like?

WHAT HAPPENS TO us after we die? I mean, there are, like, a million theories, right? "That's when we get our wings!" "We go to heaven and all live in our mansions; it's going to be amazing!" "We're just gonna be hanging out with our loved ones, floating on clouds and playing harps all day!" Yeah, yeah, yeah, I've heard it all. And I love those ideas. But what does our Bible say?

In Colossians 3 the Bible tells us we should be thinking and talking about the things of heaven, not the things of earth. Our focus should be on eternity! But the truth is, most of us know nothing about eternity. So let's obey the Word of God today and talk about eternity and what we should really be expecting.

However, if we are going to talk about eternity, that means we have to talk about judgment day too. And I know—so many people live in fear of judgment day. So I'm going to try and bring you some comfort today. Judgment day is nothing to fear if you have a relationship with Jesus. The truth is that there are actually three judgment days. The good news is, you get to pick which one you experience!

The first judgment day we have to talk about involves the great white throne of judgment. You can find this in Revelation 20:11–15. The great white throne of judgment is where you will stand before Jesus Christ seated on the throne, and He will tell you whether your name is written in the Lamb's Book of Life. What this means is that Jesus is going to ask you if you put your faith, hope, trust, and love in Him and gave your entire *life* to Him. And if you did, oh son! Your reward is great! You're going to spend *eternity* with the Father! But if your name is not found in that book, the Bible says you will spend eternity in a lake of fire. Please understand, this is a lake of fire that was never meant for you.

Now, I get it. This judgment day sounds scary. Nobody wants to hear that they're going to hell or that they're going to spend eternity in a lake of fire. But remember, I said you get to *choose* which judgment day you experience. If you've given your life to Jesus and have put your hope, faith, and entire life in His hands, *this judgment day isn't for you!*

You see, judgment day number two is only for the believer. For those who have given everything to Jesus, our judgment day already happened. It took place two thousand years ago when Jesus died on the cross, in our place. That's the greatest gift of all time because Jesus experienced that judgment for us. Do you hear what I'm saying? *We don't have to go through that judgment, because Jesus already did!* That's why I'm trying to get you to see that judgment day is nothing to be afraid of, because the price has already been paid for you!

This leads us to the third judgment day. For those whose names are in the Lamb's Book of Life, we will have *another* judgment day, when we will stand before the judgment seat of Christ, also called the bema seat of Christ. There are actually two different definitions of what the bema seat could be. The first definition is like you stepping up to a judge to receive a verdict or sentence. But the good news is that there is no verdict or sentence because Jesus paid the price and took the punishment so you wouldn't have to!

The second definition of the bema seat would be like an athlete stepping up to receive a reward or prize. (Light-bulb moment!) Aha, are you starting to get it? You see, for you and me who have already gone through judgment because we gave our lives to Jesus and received the gift He paid for us on the cross, when we stand before the bema seat, it won't be to receive judgment. It will be to receive a reward!

First Corinthians 3:13 tells us that on this judgment day, "each man's work will be revealed. For the Day will declare it, because it is revealed in *fire*; and the fire itself will test what sort of work each man's work is" (WEB, emphasis added). You see, everything you have done in this life—every action you made, every word you spoke, and every thought you let live in your mind—Jesus is going to put into a fire. What goes into that fire will either be completely burned up and destroyed or be refined like gold and have all the impurities burned away. And when Jesus pulls it back out of the fire, what's left, what's *not* burned up—that will be your reward!

Please pay attention to what one of the next verses says: "But if the work is burned up, the builder will suffer great loss. The builder will be saved, but like someone barely escaping through a wall of flames" (v. 15, NLT). What this verse is telling us is that eternity is going to look very different for each person. Whoever started the rumor that we all get a mansion and it's all going to be exactly the same for everyone clearly didn't read their Bible. This verse is telling us there are going to be some people who get into heaven by the skin of their teeth! Yeah, you got in, but you won't have much to show for it once you're there.

Think of it like this: Heaven is the most amazing concert you have ever wanted to go to. All your favorite bands are going to be there. It will have the best lights, the best smoke, the best screens, and the best sound system of all time! Everything is going to be completely incredible. But you've got to have a ticket to get in—and Jesus is that ticket.

Let me ask you something, though. Have you ever been to a concert? Is every ticket the exact same? Not at all. You see, you can get *in*to the concert and then watch the show from the TV screen in the lobby. Or you can get into the concert and have a ticket that puts you on the very back row of the nosebleed section. Or just maybe you got a decent ticket, and you're sitting in section 105. Better than that, perhaps you got a general admission ticket, and you're on the floor right in front of the stage. And let's not stop there. What if you got a backstage pass? Can it get any better than that? Oh, it absolutely can! Because maybe your ticket lets you on stage *with* the band! Do you see what I'm trying to say here?

So many people are so concerned with just getting a ticket *to* the show that they don't realize every experience is not going to be the same. I mean, if it's up to *me*, I want to sit as close to that stage as I possibly can! I want to be as close to Jesus as I can be! If eternity is going to last forever, I want it to be the best experience possible! Don't you?

"OK, so how do we *do* that, then? I want a front-row ticket too!" I'm so glad you asked! Now you're asking the right question. To answer, though, let me ask you another question. If I were to tell you that the next forty or fifty or sixty or seventy years of your life—how healthy, wealthy, and happy you are—will all be based on how you live your life over the next twenty-four hours, would that change the way you live for the next twenty-four hours? Of course it would! Look, I can't speak for you, but if you're telling me the *rest of my life* is all based on how I live the next twenty-four hours, well, then you got yourself a *perfect* man tomorrow, friend! I mean, come on! We would all do everything we possibly could in the next twenty-four hours to be as perfect as we could be, because we'd know that the rest of our lives would be determined in those twenty-four hours.

The truth is, that is what's happening to every single

person on this earth right now, and most of them have no idea whatsoever. Your entire eternity is going to be based on how you lived your life on this earth, in this moment, today. We need to start thinking of this life as a job résumé for the next. Every word you speak, every action you make, and every thought you think will go into a fire, and either it will be burned up, or you will be rewarded for it. And that reward will last forever. This life is sixty, seventy, maybe eighty years. That is short compared with eternity.

Think about this for a minute: Eternity doesn't start when you die. It starts when you give your life to Jesus. Every single day, we are building our eternity. The question is, What are you building? The Bible tells us there will be a new heaven and a new earth one day. And as much as we like to talk about living in heaven and floating with angel wings, the truth is that you and I were never created for heaven. We were made for earth. And there will come a time when we go to that new earth, and on that new earth, we will have lives, we will have jobs, and we will still have a purpose! And that all will be based on what we did here in this life. So I don't know about you, but I want to make my time here count.

Don't live in fear of judgment day. Don't live in fear of what happens when you die. If you have put your hope, trust, and faith in Jesus, you got a ticket to the show! And if you feel as if you may not have a good seat right now, the good news is you've got time to change it. If you still have breath in your lungs, it's not too late to make a change in where your ticket says you're sitting.

So again, I ask, "If the rest of your life was based on the next twenty-four hours and how you lived them, would you live differently?" Then I say we go out and start living differently. Live for Jesus with every word you speak, every thought you think, and every action you make. Build His kingdom! And when you get there, there's going to be a reward waiting for you!

CONCLUSION

MY DEAR FRIEND, you did it! You made it through twenty-five lessons that explore some of the most challenging and controversial questions we face as Christians. Let me be the first to say how proud I am of you. It would have been so much easier to shrug off these tough questions and say, "I don't know the answer. Maybe my pastor will cover that in a sermon one day." But you didn't take that route. Instead, you took on the challenge and sought out the answers for yourself. That willingness to dig deeper, to pursue understanding, truly sets you apart from many.

I sincerely pray that this book has been a blessing in your life. My hope is that it not only encouraged you but also strengthened your faith and filled you with renewed confidence in God's Word. More than anything, I pray that this book ignited a spark in you—a fire, a passion that burns brightly for the Word of God. This book was merely an appetizer, a small foretaste of the most incredible feast you could ever partake in: the Holy Bible!

Each answer I provided throughout these lessons was drawn from my personal study of God's Word. But let me be very clear, I am not special in any way. I didn't receive some secret revelation that you don't have access to. What I did, you can absolutely do as well. All I did was devote time and energy to understanding Scripture, and the same opportunity is available to every believer, including you.

I know that sometimes when we're faced with difficult or confusing parts of Scripture, it feels as though we need someone else, someone with more knowledge or experience, to explain it all to us. And to some extent, that's true. We all need mentors, pastors, and teachers to help guide us and ensure that we're interpreting the Bible correctly. God gave us spiritual leaders for a reason. However, while human teachers are important, we must never forget that the greatest teacher we have is the Holy Spirit.

I want to encourage you to keep searching for answers to those tough questions. But here's the amazing part: You don't need to wait for another book from me, or from anyone else, to find those answers. You have the most powerful resource available to you right now— God's Word! All you have to do is open your Bible, ask the Holy Spirit for guidance, and trust that He will give you understanding. As you do this, you'll be amazed at how He will enlighten your heart and mind in ways you never thought possible.

The Bible assures us that those who hunger and thirst for understanding *will* be filled. Isn't that an incredible promise? God sees your hunger for Him and His Word, and it pleases Him. He wants to speak to you. He wants to have a deep, personal relationship with you. But as we discussed earlier in this book, the Bible also tells us in James 4 that the first move is up to us. God is always there, ready and willing to meet us, but we have to take the initial step of drawing near to Him.

By reading this book, you've already taken that first step. You've shown a willingness to grow in your understanding and deepen your relationship with God. But don't stop here. This is just the beginning! There is so much more to discover, so much more truth to uncover, and so much more freedom to experience. The Bible is the most beautiful, powerful, and life-changing picture of Jesus Christ that we will ever see. As you continue to study, the Holy Spirit will reveal deeper truths to you, and you'll find yourself falling more in love with the Savior each day.

Now, I know the idea of studying the Bible on your own can feel overwhelming at times. It's a big book filled with deep, theological truths; historical context; and divine mysteries. But don't let that intimidate you. Remember, you're not studying alone. The Holy Spirit is right there with you, guiding you every step of the way. He is the ultimate Guide to understanding God's Word, and He is faithful to reveal what you need when you need it.

If you're ever unsure of where to start, let me offer some advice: Begin with prayer. Ask God to open your heart and mind to His truth. Then pick a Book of the Bible and dive in. You don't need to rush; take your time, meditate on what you're reading, and ask the Holy Spirit for clarity. If something is confusing, don't get discouraged. Use the resources available to you. Your pastor, a trusted Bible commentary, or a study group can all provide valuable insights. But remember, the Holy Spirit will be your greatest source of understanding. He knows the exact answers you're seeking, and He's eager to guide you into all truth.

One of the most amazing things about studying Scripture is that the more you read, the more you realize how much there is still to learn. God's Word is alive, and it has a way of speaking to us in new and profound ways, no matter how many times we've read the same passage. As you continue on your journey, you'll find that the Bible isn't just a book—it's a living and active conversation between God and His people. It's His way of revealing His heart, His plans, and His love to us.

So, my friend, keep going. Keep asking questions. Keep seeking truth. True freedom is found in Jesus Christ, and the Bible is the most detailed and beautiful revelation of Him that we have. Every time you open its pages, you have the opportunity to encounter the living God in a fresh and powerful way. Don't miss out on that! There is always more to learn, more to experience, and more to love about our Savior.

In closing, let me leave you with this: Never stop pursuing God. Never stop searching His Word for truth. Every answer you seek can be found in Him. And as you continue on this journey, remember that you are not alone. The Holy Spirit is with you, guiding you, teaching you, and filling you with wisdom and understanding.

Until next time, keep your heart open, your Bible in hand, and your spirit ready to receive all that God has for you. You are on an incredible journey, and I am so excited to see where God will lead you next. Love and blessings to you.

ABOUT THE AUTHOR

KELLY K IS a husband, father of five, preacher, teacher, writer, and social media missionary. Preaching the love of Jesus in a manner that is both fresh and passionate, Kelly K is a highly sought-after conference speaker and social media evangelist. Kelly K believes that social media is the largest mission field that the world has ever seen, and his messages reach out to inspire and encourage millions of lives through many multimedia platforms every single day, not just teaching them *about* Jesus but equipping them to go out and *be* the hands and feet of Jesus.

Kelly K's approach to communicating focuses on bridging the gap of cultures, ages, and societies by offering a sound that is relative to every listener or reader. So many have been blessed by the words, love, and passion of Kelly K, and thousands have come to know Jesus as their personal Lord and Savior every week by him leveraging social media for the Lord!

Kelly K currently lives in Kingfisher, Oklahoma, with his beautiful wife, Lindsay, and his five children, Brennen, Chase, Avery, Jaxx, and Jett. He is currently the associate pastor at Limitless Church of Kingfisher.